THE GOLDEN AGE *of* BALTIMORE THEATER

A History from Shakespeare to Vaudeville

CHARLIE MITCHELL

THE History PRESS

Published by The History Press
Charleston, SC
www.historypress.com

First published 2024

Manufactured in the United States

ISBN 9781467154482

Library of Congress Control Number: 2023945943

CONTENTS

PREFACE

I think I love and reverence all arts equally, only putting my own just above the others; because in it I recognize the union and culmination of them all. To me it seems as if when God conceived the world, that was Poetry; He formed it, and that was Sculpture; He colored it, and that was Painting; He peopled it with living beings, and that was the grand, divine eternal Drama.
—Charlotte Cushman, actor (1816–1876)

As a theater educator who spent many years teaching in Baltimore and enjoying the work of local theaters, I was surprised there was no survey of the city's theatrical history from its beginnings to the twentieth century. The greatest performers of every era have shared their talents to enthusiastic applause on the city's stages, and impresarios have made the city a part of their entertainment empires. As an important "tryout town," Baltimore also influenced what shows made it to Broadway. "It was generally conceded," writes historian Mildred Greenfield, "that Baltimore audiences were the most difficult ones in the country to please," an impossible claim to prove but perhaps reflective of the city's lofty standards.

No examination of the past is complete without seeing how people were entertained. Because theater deals in representation and has always been tied to the demands of the box office, it is an ideal way to explore how ideas such as ethnicity, class, gender and sexuality can be defined and redefined. The choice of piece, the length of its run and the number of revivals expose both producer and audience.

The creation of new theaters also shows how performance moves from the outskirts of culture toward its center. That is exactly what has been happening in Baltimore over the past twenty years. On Eutaw Street, the beautiful Hippodrome Theatre was renovated and is now a first-class roadhouse for national tours. The stalwart Everyman Theatre reopened in what used to be a movie house on West Fayette Street, and the Chesapeake Shakespeare Company boldly renovated a former bank on Calvert Street to create a permanent home for fans of the Bard. Institutions like Baltimore Center Stage and the Theatre Project continue to thrive, and a facility called the Motor House has been created as a new performance venue. It may be a slow trend, but considering the difficulty of raising money to create and equip a space, these developments are positive signs for the future of theater in the city and prompted me to reflect on past achievements. In doing so, my hope is to remind Baltimoreans of the power of this immediate and vibrant art form, enjoyed for so long by the inhabitants of this great city.

ACKNOWLEDGEMENTS

First and foremost, I want to thank my wife, Stephanie, for her love and support as well as her skill in keeping our four cats away from my writing desk. I am also indebted to the University of Florida's College of the Arts, which generously supported the project; David Rifkind, who was very generous with his time; and the helpful staff at the Maryland Center for History and Culture and the Jewish Museum of Maryland. I will be forever appreciative of my mother, Antonia, for her lifelong encouragement and my brother George for his willingness to traverse the streets of Baltimore to take additional photographs. Lastly, I wish to thank Kate Jenkins and Ashley Hill at The History Press for their professionalism, hard work and patience.

Illustration by Mark Watkinson.

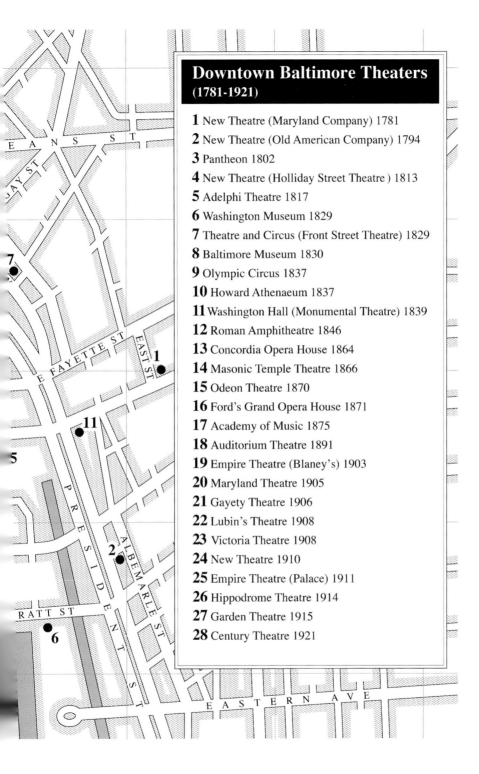

Downtown Baltimore Theaters
(1781-1921)

1 New Theatre (Maryland Company) 1781

2 New Theatre (Old American Company) 1794

3 Pantheon 1802

4 New Theatre (Holliday Street Theatre) 1813

5 Adelphi Theatre 1817

6 Washington Museum 1829

7 Theatre and Circus (Front Street Theatre) 1829

8 Baltimore Museum 1830

9 Olympic Circus 1837

10 Howard Athenaeum 1837

11 Washington Hall (Monumental Theatre) 1839

12 Roman Amphitheatre 1846

13 Concordia Opera House 1864

14 Masonic Temple Theatre 1866

15 Odeon Theatre 1870

16 Ford's Grand Opera House 1871

17 Academy of Music 1875

18 Auditorium Theatre 1891

19 Empire Theatre (Blaney's) 1903

20 Maryland Theatre 1905

21 Gayety Theatre 1906

22 Lubin's Theatre 1908

23 Victoria Theatre 1908

24 New Theatre 1910

25 Empire Theatre (Palace) 1911

26 Hippodrome Theatre 1914

27 Garden Theatre 1915

28 Century Theatre 1921

EIGHTEENTH-CENTURY BEGINNINGS

There were many who made their way in and out of populated centers in the American colonies to see if "entertainer" could be a viable occupation. Rope dancers, acrobats, ventriloquists and demonstrators of "electric fire" were periodic visitors who offered their talents for a few shillings. However, the burgeoning hamlet of Baltimore would have to wait for professional theater until the arrival of some hopeful British transplants named the Hallams. Their efforts would overcome antitheatrical sentiment and form the backbone of America theater.

THE HALLAMS

The origin of theater in Baltimore can be traced to political intrigue by a thin-skinned politician and his draconian regulation. Robert Walpole, the de facto prime minister of England, was tired of being satirized and criticized by playwrights but could not get a bill through Parliament to censor them. Subsequently, he paid the manager of a theater to claim that he was about to stage a play called *The Golden Rump*, chock-full of obscenities and treasonous attacks on the royal family. After Walpole read scandalous passages to the House of Commons, it passed his legislation known as the Licensing Act of 1737. This law gave exclusive permission to perform serious drama to only two London theater companies that did not offend the politician, Drury Lane and Covent Garden. It also required that all plays be approved by a censor. This repressive figure was the Lord Chamberlain, and he was given the power to prosecute any theater that did not seek his approval. Today, it is thought that *The Golden Rump* was Walpole's invention and the script probably never existed.

The Licensing Act was disastrous for unlicensed theaters. Desperate to survive, some managers concocted a workaround. Concerts did not require a license, and most theaters had orchestras that played before shows and during intermission. The scheme called for the rearranging of musical interludes. Patrons would buy tickets for a concert but would watch a "free play" in the middle of the program. One person who used this trick was William Hallam, the product of a large and ambitious theatrical family. His father, Thomas Hallam, was an actor whose death was one of most talked about events in London.[1] When Thomas was performing a supporting role opposite the popular actor Charles Macklin, the two quarreled backstage over who should wear a particular wig. In a fit of anger, Macklin pointed his cane at Hallam and, according to Macklin's deposition, accidentally stabbed him in the eye and pierced his brain. As Hallam lay dying, he begged for someone to urinate in his wound to disinfect it. When another actor was too horrified to oblige, Macklin did so himself.

After authorities caught on to William Hallam's concert ruse, his theater was threatened with closure. He quickly switched to free admission and high-priced alcohol, but by 1751, bankruptcy forced him to shut down. Hallam's next move would forever change the future of theater in America. Instead of starting over outside of London, where the law would have no influence, he devised a wildly audacious plan. He would outfit a group of actors, have them travel over three thousand miles to America and send his brother Lewis, an actor in his company, to lead them. This group of pioneers consisted of eleven members, along with Lewis's wife, Sarah, and their three children. Before disembarking, the actors memorized twenty-four plays, short farces and songs and rehearsed on the quarter deck of the *Charming Sally* during their six-week transatlantic voyage. Life and art mixed a little. While they were doing a scene from *The Merchant of Venice*, a porter interrupted with a plate of pork for dinner. The actor playing Shylock suddenly reeled around and dramatically bellowed, "The pound of flesh is mine; 'tis dearly bought, and I will have it!" The rattled porter dropped the dish at the actor's feet.

Calling themselves the London Company of Comedians, the troupe arrived in Yorktown in 1752 to begin touring the colonies. Regardless of whether it was intentional, the use of "London" in the troupe's name would have connected with the prevailing American mindset that everything English was of quality, while local items were intrinsically inferior. Colonists, especially those in the South, were used to being the source of raw materials that were exchanged for polished manufactured British goods. Soon, the London Company learned that no city could sustain them financially in the long term, so they moved along well-traveled roads to provincial capitals such as New York, Williamsburg, Philadelphia, Charleston and Annapolis. At the time, it would have been foolish to even consider going to sleepy Baltimore Town with its roughly two hundred inhabitants.

During their travels, the London Company was sometimes faced with great hostility from locals who were suddenly confronted with the possibility that this frivolous and decidedly English practice was finding its way into their austere colonial landscape. While practitioners touted theater as a means of transmitting virtuous behavior, its opponents equated it with cultural decay—if not outright indecency.

There had always been opposition to theater from clergy who found it to be a cesspool of moral turpitude. For example, Reverend William Law, in his tract *The Absolute Unlawfulness of the Stage-Entertainment* (1726), promoted the conservative Protestant belief that the building of permanent theaters was the same as constructing the "devil's abode, where he holds his filthy court of evil Spirits." Many colonial Puritan, Quaker and Presbyterian settlers espoused this view. Others voiced a more secular objection, which equated luxury and pleasure with corruption, evils that should be combated if the fledgling colonies were to flourish. To reject the theater was to embrace industrious colonial values.

Some even found theater to have a feminizing effect on the populace. A letter to a Pennsylvania newspaper defined it in this way: "[The theater has] an evil tendency to corrupt and debauch the mind.…When we examine the rise and fall of states, and trace the causes by which whole nations have sunk at once from the height of glory into more than Gothic barbarity, we shall find them to be principally owing to the luxury and effeminacy of the times." It is important to note that the adoption of the umbrella received much the same criticism.

Objections were also raised on economic grounds. Many used the argument that although they supported a citizen's right to attend the theater, they objected to diverting money to playgoing when other needier causes, like the building and repair of churches, hospitals and schools, were yet to be completed. Some equated money spent on theater to a tax levied against the local population. While avoiding the fact that theater going is voluntary, this specious claim ignored the boost that theater companies gave to local economies by paying local tradesmen for a variety of goods and services.

Fac simile of the Original drawing by John Moale.

BALTIMOI

Some colonial governments tried to legislate theater out of existence. Massachusetts passed the first antitheatrical ban in 1750; Pennsylvania followed suit in 1759, Rhode Island in 1761 and New Hampshire in 1762. Any amateurs who dared to present a play were hauled before local courts. In order to evade prosecution, promoters of early theatrical enterprises responded by turning to subterfuge, avoiding the use of the word *play* in favor of terms such as *lectures*, *moral dialogues* and *dissertations on subjects, moral, instructive and entertaining*. Even where theater was legal, there was no guarantee it was always welcome. It was common to send a representative to a new city or town to secure permission to perform from the local authorities. In doing so, they might be refused or have the number of performances capped in order to limit the populace's exposure. Hallam had to get a character

IN 1752.

"Baltimore Town in 1752," by John Moale. *From the New York Public Library.*

reference signed by the governor of Virginia before he could even consider embarking on a northern tour.

It was in this hostile environment that the first generation of professional actors sought to prosper. Even so, many colonists, especially those in the South, had cultural aspirations and wanted to connect with London's imagined civility and elegance. Attending the theater, as much as some wished it otherwise, was considered an urbane pastime. English actors were emissaries of polite British society, and colonists in places like Baltimore wanted to emulate their qualities while experiencing fashionable plays from London.

The "American" Company

Over time, the Hallams became the first important theatrical family in America. In London, Lewis Hallam specialized in broad physical comedy, but in America, he was admired in a variety of roles. His wife, Sarah, was considered a solid, if rather uninspired, performer. One colonial critic wrote that she was "a respectable, matron-like dame, stately or querulous as occasion required....It was absolutely necessary to forget, that to touch the heart of the spectator had any relation to her function." Their young twelve-year-old son, Lewis Jr., was destined to have an acting career but had an inauspicious debut. During the company's very first performance in America, he was cast as a servant with one line to speak, but upon seeing the audience, he erupted into tears and fled the stage. Still, Americans were impressed by Hallam's company—some even wrote poems praising specific actors—even though today, we would consider their acting style mannered and bombastic.

The Hallams sought to expand their theatrical territory by taking the company to Jamaica in 1754, but the future was uncertain after Lewis Sr. succumbed to yellow fever on the island two years later. Sarah eventually married David Douglass, the manager of another struggling troupe, and as a result of the union, the two companies merged. Led by Douglass, they traveled back to New York in 1758 and, reacting to a newly developing American identity in the colonies, rechristened the troupe the American Company of Comedians. During the next two decades, Douglass established a theatrical circuit along the Eastern Seaboard by building several permanent theaters. Their operations and the offshoots created by ex-members would go on to shape American theater for decades.

By 1772, an explosion in the flour trade, coupled with a rise in immigration, had finally made Baltimore Town a place where this new company felt they could attract a substantial audience. A playbill records a performance on June 10 in a converted stable "belonging to Mr. Little" on Frederick Street. This marks the first recorded appearance of professional theater in the city. The venue's exact location on Frederick Street was not recorded, but period newspapers make many mentions of a "Mr. John Little" who had much to do with the affairs of the town. For horse races, his stable was the place where contestants would leave certificates proving the age of their horses, and on multiple occasions, he lent his house for the public sale of various properties. Little's house was described as being "near the Market House," and at the time, there was only one market house situated on the corner of Gay and Baltimore Streets.

According to a letter printed in the *Maryland Gazette*, this Baltimore engagement was so impressive that one attendee forgot the origins of the actors: "You know I was always of opinion, that I could never sit out a play represented by American actors but I must acknowledge my error." It seems likely that the American Company played other dates, but there are no further records.

Douglass's choice of material suggests he was seeking to dispel his audience's suspicions about the immorality of the stage as well as entertain. The first work presented by the American Company was *Comus* (1634), a masque by John Milton. This was a form of courtly entertainment that included singing and dancing.[2] Written in poetic verse, it tells the story of a virtuous lady who gets lost in a forest full of spirits and rejects the hedonism of an evil sorcerer in favor of temperance and chastity. The second offering was a two-act farce written by an English clergyman called *High Life Below Stairs* (1759). "Below stairs" refers to the servants' quarters on a lower level. In the first scene, Lovel, a white, retired West Indian planter, brags to his friend that before he was ten years old, he had "a hundred blacks kissing my feet every day." Now, living in England without the free labor of enslaved people, he is convinced that his attendants are cheating him. In order to catch them in the act, the wealthy planter borrows a costume from a theater manager friend and disguises himself as a poor country servant. Soon, he discovers that his employees are a pack of thieving drunkards, and the play ends with them receiving their comeuppance. *High Life Below Stairs* can be seen as a prime example of the class antagonism between employers and servants found in documents throughout the century. It was common for employers to complain about paying high wages and grumble about familiarity and insubordination. There is also evidence of backlash from the servant class, who did not appreciate being painted with so wide a brush. When the play premiered in Edinburgh, there was a gallery reserved for footmen who, angered over the satirical portrayal of their profession, rioted and were permanently ejected from the theater.

This play is also notable for its inclusion of two Black characters, a "kitchen wench" and a footman, clearly from the master's former life in the West Indies. Their presence means that the city's first professional performance most likely included actors in blackface. This practice reinforced the idea that white actors were a blank canvas on whom any race could be painted with makeup. Although this is considered distasteful today, it continued mostly unchallenged well into the twentieth century.

Douglass had shown himself to be a very capable manager. Politically, he was especially skillful in not taking sides between the Americans and the British. He rubbed elbows with revolutionaries and theater-lovers George Washington and Thomas Jefferson but also used British soldiers to fill out the cast of plays when the company played in New York. He also dined with royal governors and other members of high society with strong ties to England. However, there was no avoiding the Revolutionary War, which would change the fortunes of the company and jeopardize their possibility of creating a lasting theatrical presence in Baltimore. In 1774, the Continental Congress banned public amusements and extravagances during this time of sacrifice. With their livelihood criminalized, Douglass and his company boarded one of the last ships to leave New York and sailed back to Jamaica to sit out the conflict. When the company resumed operations, the island was still a British possession, and most of the audiences they entertained were composed of military men. For Douglass, an audience was an audience.

Four years later, the Continental Congress, responding to violations of its original bill, reiterated its prohibition of play-going:

> *Whereas true religion and good morals are the only solid foundations of public liberty and happiness: Resolved, That it be and it is hereby earnestly recommended to the several states to take the most effectual measures for the encouragement thereof, and for the suppressing theatrical entertainments, horse-racing, gaming, and other such diversions as are productive of idleness, dissipation, and a general depravity of principles and manners.*

This was no doubt a response to George Washington allowing soldiers to stage plays while encamped at Valley Forge, a move that mirrored the British army's theatrical activities. Three days later, another resolution stated that "any person holding an office under the United States" would be dismissed if they "act, promote, encourage, or attend such plays." The bill passed over the objections of Maryland and other states. This meant that theater in Baltimore would be on hiatus until one eager entrepreneur decided to strike out on his own.

THOMAS WALL

In 1781, four months before the conclusion of the war at Yorktown, Thomas Wall, an actor formerly with the American Company, came to Baltimore with his wife and daughter, hoping to organize his own theater company. In London, Wall had been a comic actor specializing in humorous valets and only played minor roles in America. During the eighteenth and nineteenth centuries, actors had "lines of business." In other words, when a play was chosen to perform, each actor in the company would have ownership of a character type. These included the leading lady and leading man, ingénue and male juvenile lead, walking lady or gentleman (secondary parts), light comedian (funny gentleman), low comedian (funny men of low social station), "the heavy" (villain), soubrette (female maids and servants) and general utility players (or "utes"), as needed. Once a line of business was established, it was common for actors to be very possessive of it, which led to some comic outcomes. There is one story from England about an actress who played a virgin while nine months pregnant.

Wall sought to break this theatrical caste system and transform himself into a leading man. After receiving permission from Maryland's state council, he began by performing a modest program going back and forth between an Annapolis theater and a Baltimore coffeehouse, sail warehouse and dancing room. His performance consisted of various prologues and epilogues, common in plays of that period, as well as comical lectures. One referenced in a playbill was undoubtedly *The Lecture on Heads*, one of the most popular and pirated pieces of the era. Using a display of paper-mâché heads, a performer would point to each one and talk about its personality type. This allowed him to satirize figures, such as child prodigies, busybodies, ladies of fashion, ministers and quack doctors. To pull the heartstrings of the audience, Wall also had his seven-year-old daughter sing while he accompanied her on a mandolin and ended by performing a monologue from a Shakespearean play. Heartened by the response, he got local backing and advertised for actors in the *Maryland Journal*. The construction of a brick theater on what is now East Baltimore Street (between East and Lloyd Streets) began during the winter and was completed by mid-January. Known simply as the New Theatre, or Baltimore Theatre, it was the first permanent theater in the city.

Wall's financial managers were an innkeeper and a merchant, amateurs who, by virtue of their talent or their pocketbooks, became actors according to the surviving playbills. We do not know the exact size of the theater but based on box office receipts for its best attended evening, it had at least 789 seats. Despite Wall's advertisement assuring a "well-Regulated" theater, a petition signed by thirty-seven citizens was sent to the governor, protesting the theater's existence but to no avail. Wall's company, newly christened the Maryland Company of Comedians, would be the first permanent acting company in Baltimore and the first one in the colonies since the beginning of the Revolution.

Colonial theater might have seemed foreign to us in many ways. Unlike today's fan-shaped seating, colonial theaters used a rectangular English configuration called a "box, pit and gallery," common since the seventeenth century. It was a rectangular room with a small, raised stage on one end, and facing the stage were rows of wooden benches for seating (the pit), the area we call the orchestra today. This was the place for unattached men of fashion; allowing women there was considered a sign of a disreputable establishment. On the sides of the room were slightly raised seats for wealthier patrons (boxes). Finally, there was raised seating in the back of the auditorium (gallery) for the poorer, working-class patrons, what we would call the balcony. Theater seating has always been one of the ultimate expressions of class distinction, and in the colonies, money created the new aristocracy. Before the curtain, servants were sent to hold seats of their employers, another clear signifier of economic prosperity.

This was a period of representation, not realism. When it came to design, no effort was made at historical accuracy. Actors were expected to provide many of their own costumes. One surviving letter to a theater manager recommends an actress because of her extensive wardrobe, not her acting skills. When it came to settings, a small number of painted canvas backdrops were used to indicate, not duplicate, whatever location was referenced in the play (a pastoral setting, a drawing room, a castle, et cetera). These were so important that advertising a new painted backdrop was a way to increase ticket sales. As for lighting, no effort was made to darken the house during performances in order to heighten the reality on stage. Both the audience and the stage were illuminated by foul-smelling tallow candles, which would often drip on actors and patrons in the pit.

Eighteenth-century audiences could not be faulted for their lack of stamina. Performances could last from four to six hours. Wall had a small company of six men and three women (Wall's wife played mostly male parts). They performed two shows a week, usually on Tuesdays and Fridays. It was illegal to hold performances on Sunday, since church attendance was still mandatory during this period.[3] The evenings began at 6:00 p.m. A play was

The John Street Theatre in New York (1791), an example of a simple box, pit and gallery configuration. *From the New York Public Library Digital Collections.*

commonly followed by an afterpiece, a short comic play, and music and/or dance interludes were performed between plays. The material comprised tried and true plays from the English repertoire, adapted Shakespeare and contemporary farces. Copyright was in its infancy, and early laws that were adopted did not include plays. It was believed that once a play was performed, it became the property of those who heard it. This made piracy commonplace. Theaters would send agents to successful plays to write down the dialogue so it could be duplicated, which discouraged playwriting as a means to make a living.

Richard III was the Maryland Company's first offering, with Wall performing the role of the treacherous prince. This was a safe choice, as Shakespeare was a literary favorite in the colonies. It is likely the company would have used the abbreviated and rewritten version of Shakespeare's play that had been in use since 1700. A dusty afterpiece followed titled *A Miss in Her Teens*, a thirty-five-year-old farce by famed British actor David Garrick. At the opening performance, Wall's curtain speech to his new audience portrayed both a nervous optimism and a nagging sense of dread:

From Shakespeare's golden mines we'll fetch the ore
And land these riches here in Baltimore;
For we theatric merchants never quit
His boundless shores of universal wit.
But we in vain shall richly laden come
Unless deep water brings us safely home;
Unless your favor in full tides will flow,
Ship, crew and cargo to the bottom go!

Even though Wall attempted to cast his company as cultural emissaries bearing gifts, the "favor" he so badly craved would be difficult to realize. Despite a public relations blitz that sold the theater as a place of gentility, refinement and virtue, the house was often half full. He also experienced the pitfalls of a town unused to the rules of decorum in a theater. In one newspaper pronouncement, Wall threatened "exemplary punishment" to the "several evil-disposed persons" who threw apples and bottles on the stage during a performance.

Wall tried, in many ways, to ingratiate himself with his public. In 1782, the company presented *Gustavus Vasa*, a play that was banned in England, the first casualty of the Licensing Act. It was dedicated to "George Washington as deliverer of the country" and depicted the leader of the Swedish struggle for freedom from Denmark in the sixteenth century. No one in the audience could have missed the comparison to American political dissent when the character of Vasa called his soldiers "sons of liberty." Wall also attempted to curry favor with the locals by holding benefits for charity and donating money for street repairs. One of the largest impediments to the company's success was the town's treacherous unpaved roads and wooden bridges. Wall also allowed members of the community to appear in plays "for their own amusement." Most likely, the appearance of these locals was done in exchange for a fee, a common practice that allowed for a more invested local audience, as well as a source of much-needed income.

For a gallery seat, the Maryland Company charged nine pence, a seat in the pit cost five shillings and a box seat cost one dollar. The playbill advertising these prices probably refers to a Spanish milled dollar, which was worth up to eight shillings. During his second season, Wall changed his policy to a five-shilling flat fee. To measure the expense of an evening of entertainment, consider that one or two shillings could buy you a meal at a tavern, twelve could buy a bushel of corn and, tragically, an enslaved person under the age of eight might be valued at two hundred shillings.

Pit and gallery tickets were rarely sold at theaters. Instead, they could be purchased at a printer's shop, tavern or coffeehouse. Box seats could be purchased at the theater but were usually picked up by servants who were sent by their employers. Impossible to omit is the name of the printer of theatrical playbills in Baltimore at the time, the intrepid and accomplished Mary Katharine Goddard. Not only was she the postmaster general and publisher of the *Maryland Journal*, but she was also responsible for the second printing of the Declaration of Independence, the first with the printed names of the signers.

Wall had strict rules for his troupe. Fines between five and thirty shillings were charged for breaking any backstage rules, such as missing rehearsal, not putting a costume away or powdering hair in the dressing room. Since the pay they received was modest, actors could be awarded a benefit, a single evening's performance where they received all the box office proceeds after paying for the rental of the theater and the other actors. A benefit could net an actor more money than they could make in a year as a member of the acting company. Wall was unusual in that he broke from the English system of awarding benefits solely to leading actors and adopted a more democratic approach by holding a lottery.

Perhaps weary of the day-to-day pressures of managing a theater, Wall hired a new manager named Dennis Ryan, a veteran actor from Ireland, who took over the company in 1783. Meanwhile, Wall continued to perform major roles with the company. Based on the distribution of parts, this transition between managers did not seem to be disruptive. According to box office receipts, the most successful play among Baltimore audiences during Ryan's tenure was George Lillo's *The London Merchant*, the story of a young, innocent apprentice who is corrupted by a local prostitute and then murders his beloved uncle. The play has the usual obsession with morality that was typical of this era, but it also indicated a cultural shift by relocating the subject of tragedy from the upper classes to the middle and working classes, an example of their increasing influence.

It is difficult to determine the overall quality of these nascent theatrical pioneers. Notices by Wall seeking actors indicate his casts were fleshed out with amateurs who did not respect the written word. Before Ryan took over, the *Maryland Journal* complained that "the players have taken it into their heads, that the plays which they act are not witty enough in themselves, and that they require to be spiced with their own wit to make them more palatable" and that "our players are degenerating into a group of obscene blunderers and abominable interpolators."

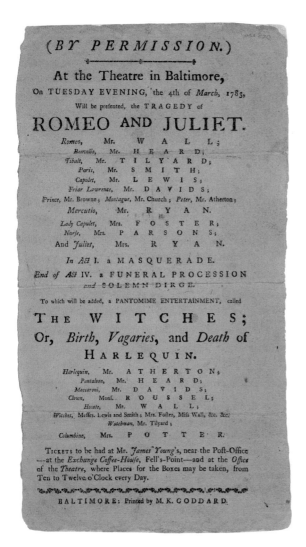

(BY PERMISSION.)

At the Theatre in Baltimore,
On TUESDAY EVENING, the 4th of *March*, 1783,
Will be presented, the TRAGEDY of

ROMEO AND JULIET.

Romeo, Mr. W A L L ;
Benvolio, Mr. H E A R D ;
Tibalt, Mr. T I L Y A R D ;
Paris, Mr. S M I T H ;
Capulet, Mr. L E W I S ;
Friar Lawrence, Mr. D A V I D S ;
Prince, Mr. Browne ; Montague, Mr. Church ; Peter, Mr. Atherton ;
Mercutio, Mr. R Y A N.

Lady Capulet, Mrs. F O S T E R ;
Nurse, Mrs. P A R S O N S ;
And Juliet, Mrs. R Y A N.

In Act I. a M A S Q U E R A D E.
End of Act IV. a FUNERAL PROCESSION
and SOLEMN DIRGE.

To which will be added, a PANTOMIME ENTERTAINMENT, called

THE WITCHES;

Or, *Birth, Vagaries,* and *Death* of
H A R L E Q U I N.

Harlequin, Mr. A T H E R T O N ;
Pantaloon, Mr. H E A R D ;
Maccaroni, Mr. D A V I D S ;
Clown, Monf. R O U S S E L ;
Hecate, Mr. W A L L ;
Witches, Meſſrs. Lewis and Smith ; Mrs. Foſter, Miſs Wall, &c. &c.
Watchman, Mr. Tilyard ;

Columbine, Mrs. P O T T E R.

TICKETS to be had at Mr. *James Young's*, near the Poſt-Office
----at the *Exchange Coffee-Houſe,* Fell's-Point----and at the *Office*
of the *Theatre,* where Places for the Boxes may be taken, from
Ten to Twelve o'Clock every Day.

BALTIMORE: Printed by M. K. GODDARD.

A Maryland Company playbill. *From the Folger Shakespeare Library Digital Image Collection.*

By the 1780s, Baltimore's population had grown from six thousand to eleven thousand since the Hallams' first visit, but even with the Maryland Company providing a new repertory of plays every month—a total of twenty-one serious plays and twelve farces in four years—a full-time company was still difficult to sustain. After they attempted a brief tour, on which they were misleadingly labeled the American Company of Comedians, Ryan's poor health and subsequent death in 1786 seemed to doom any chance of continuing the enterprise. As for Wall, one story claims that he remained in Baltimore and attempted to open a school for fencing, while another says he traveled south to teach music. The fate of Wall's Baltimore theater is unknown, but perhaps its disappearance from historical records suggests the building was not of sufficient quality to attract any other theatrical endeavors.

Wall's efforts launched the careers of many actors, but perhaps his greater accomplishment was providing a great stride toward normalizing theater in Baltimore as a cultural fact, not an exotic indulgence. Around this time, a London paper said that Americans were developing a taste for theatricals, a fact that no doubt persuaded many actors that this new country could be fertile ground for practicing their art and making their fortunes.

THE NEW OLD AMERICAN COMPANY

Back in Jamaica, Lewis Hallam Jr. took over the management of the American Company after his mother died and his stepfather retired. Now in his forties, he had spent most of his life in the theater and was a leading man. Up to this point, Hallam had played a large number of leading roles, including Romeo (to his mother's Juliet!) and Hamlet in what was possibly the first showing of Shakespeare's play in the United States. With the Revolution over, Hallam reorganized his players and returned to the United States in 1785. Seeking to remind audiences of previous tours and to call out imitators, the troupe was renamed the Old American Company. Despite being an accomplished actor, Hallam was known to be contentious and inept when it came to money matters.[4] Perhaps recognizing his shortcomings, he designated a comanager named John Henry, an Irish actor who specialized in "serious and pathetic fathers."

In 1786, Henry decided to build a new theater in Baltimore. During the Revolution, the town had become a crucial shipbuilding port, and along with its extensive trade with the West Indies, it was on its way to becoming a promising commercial city. As a result, it now had the makings of a prime theatrical destination.

The area Henry chose for the theater was Philpot's Hill, which overlooked Fell's Point. It was an open common named for a wealthy family who had large real estate holdings in the city. The landlord at this time was probably former Continental army veteran Brian Philpot Jr. or one of his agents. According to one account, Henry reached an agreement "over a bottle," which said that the company could lease the land in exchange for fifteen free box seats every year. Construction of the New Theatre was finished in 1786, and the only surviving description called it a large wood-frame building.

For four years, the Old American Company included Baltimore in their touring schedule. Their number of visits even eclipsed Annapolis, the first American city to build a permanent theater, and were almost equal to their number of visits to New York. The plays they presented were mostly light fare. The two that appeared the most were *The Rivals* (1775) and *The School for Scandal* (1777), written by the widely admired Richard Brinsley Sheridan. Both are comedies of manners in which upper-class libertines behave badly while speaking witty dialogue, prime examples of work written after 1660, when the monarchy was restored in England.

Eliza Tuke, an actress and the second wife of Lewis Hallam Jr. *From the Folger Shakespeare Library Digital Image Collection.*

Another play in their repertoire that is worthy of mention is Isaac Bickerstaffe's short comic opera *The Padlock* (1768), the story of a man who locks up his fiancée for fear of becoming a cuckhold. The piece includes a character called Mungo, a lazy and gullible West Indian servant played in blackface. Thomas Wall had played the character multiple times, but it was Lewis Hallam Jr.'s portrayal that garnered great admiration, probably for moments like the following in which Mungo bemoans his life of servitude in a broad dialect:

> *Dear heart, what a terrible life am I led,*
> *A dog has a better that's shelter'd and fed:*
> *Night and day 'tis de same,*
> *My pain is dere game;*
> *Me wish to de Lord me was dead.*
> *What e'er's to be done,*
> *Poor black must run;*
> *Mungo here, Mungo dere,*
> *Mungo every where;*
> *Above and below,*
> *Sirrah come, Sirrah go,*
> *Do so, and do so.*
> *Oh! oh!*
> *Me wish to de Lord me was dead.*

Despite these glimpses of humanity, the opera avoids the moral implications of slavery by keeping Mungo a comic device. Due to the opera's popularity in Europe and the Americas, *Mungo* became a generic term for any enslaved person.

The last recorded performance of the Old American Company in Baltimore occurred in October 1790. Thereafter, they concentrated on New York and seemingly did not return. In a letter, Hallam suggested that the Baltimore theater was not ideally situated or profitable and perhaps easy to abandon:

> *The theatre, which Henry by a Gross Error in Judgement has so Plac'd that even in the Best of Weather it must be attended with the greatest inconvenience to the Audience, but in bad its Distance and Situation render it almost impractical to come at—a Deluge of Rain, which has Continued to fall, ever since the Theatre open'd has so much hurt the Business that out of 7 Performances only one has reached a 100L* [pounds].

Despite Hallam's exit, his Baltimore theater would not go dark. Various companies would temporarily fill the void.

The first was the French Company of Comedians in 1790. The group was probably composed of Acadians, people who resided in Nova Scotia just before the French and Indian War. Since they refused to sign a loyalty oath to Great Britain, they were forcibly relocated to various colonies. One thousand were transported to Maryland, and the governor, concerned about providing services to so many refugees, divided them among various communities, including Baltimore. It is likely that the actors were descended from this group and resided in an area called French-town, centered on the corner of Pratt and Charles Streets.

One of the plays presented by this French company was *La Jeune Indienne* (1764), a one-act comedy written in verse by French playwright Sébastien-Roch Nicolas Chamfort. Advertised as *The Indian in Charleston, or, The Savagesse* [*sic*], the action of the play takes place after an English officer named Belton is shipwrecked on an island and is saved by Betti, a Native woman. They soon fall in love and manage to signal a passing vessel, which takes them back to his home in Charleston. The officer's home was moved from England to Charleston when the play was shown in that city. Feeling his duty and the threat of poverty, Belton decides he must submit to a marriage that was arranged by his father, but in the end, Belton's father sees the love his son feels for the Native woman and arranges their wedding. Although he planned to visit, Chamfort never traveled to America or the

Alexandre Placide. *From the Harvard Theatre Collection, Houghton Library, Harvard University.*

West Indies, where the play is set. As a result, the character of Betti is a classic example of "the noble savage" stock character, depicted as industrious and living in an uncorrupted state of nature. On the stage, authors tended to either romanticize Native people or portray them as savage killers to be feared.

In 1791, the next occupant of the theater was the troupe of Frenchman Alexandre Placide, who claimed to be the "first rope dancer to the King of France." He was a celebrity in Europe, and his acrobatic prowess was so legendary that he was given the nickname "the great Devil." He had been acquitted of a kidnapping charge in France, but with his reputation sullied, he decided to settle in Saint Domingue, a French colony in the Caribbean. There, he met thirteen-year-old Suzanne Vaillande, a classically trained ballerina whose family had fled the turmoil of the French Revolution. After she joined Placide's company and became his mistress, a 1791 slave rebellion drove the two to Baltimore for their first American performances. Placide, Vaillande (sometimes incorrectly advertised as Madame Placide) and three other performers presented mostly pantomimes.

Pantomime was a theatrical form featuring the comic servant Harlequin, filled with dance, acrobatics, fencing and tightrope dancing. It was the result of an Italian comedy invasion of Europe that began in the sixteenth century called commedia dell'arte. This semi-improvised masked form became so popular that it came to dominate theater in France. The Comédie-Française, the national theater, was so tired of this competition that it obtained an injunction to ban the spoken word in theaters run by foreigners. Consequently, the wily Italians adapted their plays so they could be acted without speaking and underscored them with music. This new form called pantomime (or "panto") created a sensation the French and English emulated. Later, it would become much more formalized and elaborate, but during this time, it provided a narrative framework for Placide and Vaillande to showcase their acrobatic and dancing skills.

After leaving Baltimore, Placide and Vaillande joined the Old American Company for a time and were later important figures in the theater scene in

Madame Placide in the ballet *The Bird Catcher*, 1792. *From the New York Public Library*.

Charleston. However, their partnership was threatened when they played in Boston and an attractive male dancer joined the troupe. When he began to court Vaillande, a jealous Placide challenged him to a duel. The lovestruck dancer lost and suffered a slight wound, but Vaillande chose to marry him instead of staying with Placide. Vaillande would not allow her marriage to stop her career. She would go on to become the first woman choreographer in the United States.

The next resident of Hallam's theater came in 1793, when two actors tried to create a resident theater company, the first in Baltimore since Thomas Wall. William Godwin, formerly of the American Company, had previously opened his own theater in Savannah after the Revolution and participated in the creation of another theater in Charleston. To test the theatrical waters in Baltimore, he had already done two solo appearances a year earlier, which included the ubiquitous *The Lecture on Heads*, "a humorous oration," and a poetic tribute to George Washington. Along with another actor he knew in Charleston, Christopher Charles McGrath, he formed a company and used the abandoned name of the Maryland Company. Besides Godwin and McGrath, only two other actors in the company seemed to have been professionals. Nevertheless, they were prolific, offering an entire season of plays, with Godwin in leading roles and McGrath in supporting ones.

Later that same year, Godwin and McGrath posted a notice that the theater was closed until new company members could be located. The reopening never happened. Although there is some evidence of a falling out between Godwin and McGrath, what killed the chance of a lasting resident company was likely a major outbreak of yellow fever. It first appeared around the docks of Fell's Point, infecting sailors, laborers, tradesmen and their families. Unfortunately, the city was slow to react. Class prejudice from officials led them to mistakenly blame the early deaths on a combination of heat and drunkenness. A Baltimore doctor, frustrated by the city's tepid response to the epidemic, wrote in 1794 that in one day, twenty-three died, many within twelve hours of being infected. As a result, the streets of Fell's Point were deserted, and Baltimoreans left the city in droves to escape the risk of infection. An English visitor grimly described contractors being paid three dollars per corpse to put the infected dead in communal graves. Also, coffins were placed next to the bedsides of the dying to expedite their funerals. It was this haste in disposing of the bodies that led to persistent rumors that some people were being buried alive.

WIGNELL AND THE HOLLIDAY STREET THEATRE

Another permanent theater would come to be built in Baltimore through the efforts of a popular actor named Thomas Wignell. The cousin of Lewis Hallam Sr., he joined the Old American Company in 1774, just before the theaters were closed by the Continental Congress. When the company returned, he was a featured player and shared a limited leadership role. One critic described him as a "comic actor, not a buffoon," a man whose comedy was "luxuriant in humour, but always faithful to his author."

The "author" mentioned by the critic would have certainly been British, since their plays would dominate American theater well into the nineteenth century. Only a few Americans attempted to bring their voices to the stage. In 1784, a Philadelphian named Peter Markoe presented his play *The Patriot Chief* to Lewis Hallam Jr. in the hopes that the company would produce it. Stiffly written in blank verse, it was the story of a revolution against the king of Lydia, the leader of an ancient kingdom. Despite being an obvious reference to the Revolution, Lewis Jr. passed. Another American named Royall Tyler was more successful. When the Old American Company was in New York, it presented *The School for Scandal*, which was seen and admired by Tyler, a lawyer and former major in the Continental army. Inspired to write his own comedy of manners and encouraged by Wignell, Tyler penned *The Contrast*, which was presented by the company in April 1787 and added to their repertory. This would be the first comedy by an American professionally staged in Baltimore and the first American play to be seen in the city. Wignell, who was given the copyright of the play by Tyler, was so proud of his discovery that he privately published it and sent two copies to George Washington.

The Contrast takes its title from the comparison between the vanities of fashion and American virtue. The opening prologue, spoken by Wignell, seemed to herald a new age of republican representation on the stage:

> *EXULT, each patriot heart!—this night is shewn*
> *A piece, which we may fairly call our own;*
> *Where the proud titles of "My Lord! Your Grace!"*
> *To humble Mr. and plain Sir give place.*

Set in New York, the plotless script is a stylistic copy of Sheridan but has some touches of quality like this wonderfully self-referential exchange between two servants, Jenny and a plain-spoken Yankee bumpkin named Jonathan:

> *Jenny: So, Mr. Jonathan, I hear you were at the play last night.*
> *Jonathan: At the play! Why, do you think I went to the devil's drawing room?*
> *Jenny: The devil's drawing room?*
> *Jonathan: Yes; why, ain't cards and dice the devil's device, and the play-house the shop where the devil hangs out the vanities of the world upon*

the tenter-hooks of temptation? I believe you have not heard how they were acting the old boy one night, and the wicked one came among them, sure enough, and went right off in a storm, and carried one quarter of the play-house with him. Oh no, no, no! You won't catch me at a play-house, I warrant you.

Wignell was celebrated for his performance of Jonathan, and once popularized, the Yankee figure would appear in dozens of other plays. However, it was not Tyler's invention. It was the theatrical realization of "Brother Jonathan," a fictional New England character who had already appeared in print for some time. What is not widely known is that the appearance of "Brother Jonathan," with his striped pants and waistcoat, would later become the template for Uncle Sam, the personification of the U.S. government.

Angered over not being given the assignment to return to London to recruit more actors, Wignell brazenly broke from the company in 1791 and took the trip anyway, determined to start his own troupe. He returned a year later with a group of fifty-six actors, musicians, backstage crew and their families, along with costumes and painted scenery. Actors with large families were generally looked on favorably. Children could fill out a cast when the need arose, a practice that created many generational acting dynasties. Wignell also stole select actors from Hallam's company to fill out his troupe.

Wignell found wealthy patrons in Philadelphia and built the Chestnut Street Theatre in 1794, but his plans were much greater than opening a single theater. Having worked under Hallam, he understood that a successful touring company needed control over its venues. That same year, Wignell traveled to Baltimore along with his partner, well-known musician Alexander Reinangle, and bought land to build another theater on Holliday Street, named for its owner, Robert Holliday. In order to raise funds, shares of $100 were sold, along with a guarantee of 6 percent interest until the debt was paid. The *Maryland Journal* proclaimed that the "inhabitants of Baltimore and its vicinity will soon have the opportunity of being gratified with the most refined and rational amusement

A portrait of Thomas Wignell, 1792. *From George Charles Williamson,* John Russell, R.A. *(London: George Bell & Sons, 1894), 131.*

which a liberal mind is capable of enjoying." Once built, the wooden structure was described as "the New Theatre."[5]

Wignell's company played summer and autumn seasons there, presenting three performances a week. Once established, this Holliday Street venue would become part of a southern circuit of theaters that included Philadelphia, Annapolis, Washington and Alexandria, Virginia, and go on to become the city's most treasured theatrical institution.[6] Many called it the Old Drury, a nickname borrowed from a beloved theater on London's Drury Lane.

Perhaps the theater's best description comes from a Maryland novelist, John P. Kennedy, who remembered it quite fondly: "What a superb thing it was!—speaking now as my fancy imagined it then. It had something of the splendor of a great barn, weather-boarded, milk-white, with many windows; and to my conception, looked with a hospitable, patronizing, tragi-comic greeting down upon the street." He goes on to recount the reception received by the actors:

> *There was a universal gladness in this old Baltimore when the word was passed round—"The players are come." It instantly became everybody's business to give them a good reception.…We ran after them in the streets as something very notable to be looked at.…The chief actors were invited into the best company, and I believe personal merits entitled them to all the esteem that was felt for them. But, among the young folks, the appreciation was far above all this. With them it was a kind of hero-worship, prompted by a conviction that the player was that manifold creature which every night assumed a new shape, and only accidentally fell into the category of a common mortal.*

Even allowing for nostalgia's rose-colored glasses, the company undoubtedly made an impression.

By 1796, Baltimore Town had experienced remarkable growth. Business was booming, mainly because of the city's port, which had strong connections to Europe and the Caribbean. As a result, the complexities of Baltimore's civil administration could no longer be effectively handled by state commissioners. A charter was passed, and Jones Town and Fell's Point were incorporated into the new City of Baltimore. At the same time, this growth came with a desire for more control. A year later, the newly formed City Council of Baltimore, in an effort to curtail "idleness, dissipation and a depravity of principles," passed an ordinance that said all performers had to purchase a license from the mayor for each showing. Violators would be fined $1,000, an outrageous sum that was more symbolic of municipal power than a practical punishment. The new rule also prohibited performances between June and October, a tremendous blow to Wignell's business. His protests to the city were ignored, and as a result, there were years in which the theater was entirely dark. With a stroke of a pen, the city council curtailed the growth of theater in the city well into the next century. In a 1799 letter, William Osborn Payne, a rabid theater fan living in Baltimore, wrote of Wignell's company: "There are but few good Players among them and they are badly encouraged."

The colonial period was a time of great optimism. For some enterprising British managers and actors, the promise of America was too enticing to pass up, an opportunity to recreate themselves and find new audiences. It was also a time of great instability. Monetary and logistical hardships, along with heavy regulation, assured that Baltimore would soon go from a theatrical suburb of Annapolis to an extension of Philadelphia's theater interests. In the next century, there would be many stops and starts before the Monumental City would go on to rival cities like New York as an artistic destination.

2

MELODRAMA AND MINSTRELSY

By 1800, Baltimore had become the third-largest city in the country. It had twenty-six thousand residents and 130 busy streets, and along with its rapid growth, it needed places for socializing outside the home. For the average citizen, the city's one hundred taverns provided that space. For the elite, company could be found in assembly rooms, halls that provided opportunities to drink refreshments, gamble at cards and dance. By 1797, there was such a demand that a building was constructed at the northeast corner of Fayette and Holliday Streets, the elegant Baltimore Assembly Rooms, at the cost of $38,000. It was designed by former Continental army colonel Nicholas Rogers, who used twenty-five-year-old Robert Cary Long Sr. as what we would call a general contractor today.[7] This would be valuable experience for young Long, who would become an important Maryland architect.

Selling memberships to these rooms guaranteed exclusivity, and the aristocracy of Baltimore rose to the occasion by wearing their best. Arriving in expensive carriages or on horseback, men in powdered wigs, cravats and short breeches mingled with women who had elaborate pyramids of hair and wore taffeta dresses with long trains. Decorum was always followed, and the inebriated were removed. Certain customs surrounding these assemblies were uniquely American. For example, blank cards were not manufactured in the United States, so invitations to balls were written on the backs of playing cards.

Theatrical entertainment was often included at these assembly halls. In 1802, a Mr. Bier managed a room that contained a small theater, which accommodated about 150 people. In 1809, "Mr. Barnet's Assembly-Room" showcased a solo performance by John Howard Payne. Payne was an eighteen-year-old actor who had become such a sensation that he was called "the American Roscius," a comparison to a renowned actor of ancient Rome.[8] After performing in the city for twelve consecutive nights, Payne earned the handsome sum of $1,500.[9] One newspaper exclaimed:

All those who from Payne had experienced delight,
With increased admiration and pleasure each night,
To evince their desire of delighting again,
Attended last night, and gave pleasure to Payne![10]

JOHN HOWARD PAYNE Esq

John Howard Payne as Hamlet. *From the Folger Shakespeare Library Digital Image Collection.*

Another burst with pride: "I honour genius and worth, wherever and in whomsoever they may be found; but in an American I almost adore them. It adds something to a man's own importance, (especially in his own estimation), when he can stand up before an admiring world, and say of an extraordinary genius—He is my countryman!"

These appearances were part of Payne's successful southern tour before work became scarce and he departed for England in 1812, a voyage funded by his admirers in Baltimore. It is believed that he was the first professional American actor to appear on the British stage. In his long career, he also wrote over sixty works, but he is now remembered only for the lyrics of the song "Home Sweet Home," which were borrowed from one of his operas.

THE PLEASURE GARDEN

The growth of Baltimore led many to desire an escape from its faster pace and noise. Enter pleasure gardens, a number of privately owned manicured parks that could be found in most major American cities. Mainly, the gardens attracted those who could not afford country houses and wanted to escape the heat, mingle or romance under shaded walkways. For an admission fee, people could leisurely enjoy nature, refreshments, snacks, civic meetings and, sometimes, performances. For nighttime strolls, ladies wore evening dresses and men walked with hats under their arms as lamps or torches lit the way. These gardens provided a space where one could perform gentility against the roughness of the city landscape. Unfortunately, gentility was sometimes in short supply. A rash of pickpocketing and destruction of property led to the introduction of constables to watch over the customers.

On the corner of what is now East Baltimore and North Bond Streets was the site of the Columbia Garden. This is where Pennsylvania-born John Durang, a dancer, actor and singer, was contracted by the owner to build and manage a temporary theater in 1805. As a young man, Durang had seen Thomas Wall's company perform and became determined to take the stage. He eventually joined Hallam's company and played in Baltimore in 1790. Playbills indicate that he was utilized mostly as a featured dancer between plays, but when he switched to Wignell's Philadelphia troupe, he was given supporting roles. His experience in both companies gave him the confidence to strike out on his own. During the summer, when the theater was inactive, he would pack his family and a few other actors into a wagon and tour through Pennsylvania Dutch country and other areas, playing hotels, ballrooms and coffeehouses. No doubt his time at the theater on Holliday Street convinced him a Baltimore engagement could be profitable.

Durang improved the Columbia Garden by creating "a stage with a cover, a curtain with the decorations of scenery," and "a circus ring was formed between the stages and the boxes," as was "an elevated gallery." Likely a makeshift affair, the stage was used for plays and other entertainments, while the ring was utilized for equestrian acts, like chasing clowns in comic sequences or jumping through a hogshead of fire. The garden was officially outside of the city and could avoid the city's ban on summer theater. Durang's salary was fifty dollars a week with a "clear benefit," a reference to a single performance in which he could keep all the proceeds and management would pick up the additional costs. This was a princely sum when you consider that even skilled workers made just over one dollar a day.

Durang's opening night was a disaster. The musicians were not on time, and the crowd demolished the stage in protest while the actors ran away. Despite this setback, Durang wrote that the rest of the season was heavily attended and quite lucrative. Audiences responded positively to the variety of acts he provided, something halfway between theater and circus. A typical night might have included a ballet, trick riding, music, a short play, a specialty dance, pantomimes, gymnastics and fireworks to cap the evening. During the summer of 1805, Durang and his small troupe gave twenty-six performances on Mondays and Thursdays.

The following year, he became displeased with the management of the garden and moved to a new space called the Pantheon on Calvert Street. This octagonal building was near what was eventually called the Northern Fountain, one of several springs that provided water to the city but was later covered by new construction. It was built in 1802 to "display a panoramic view consisting of paintings measuring 150 feet portraying patriotic subjects" and was used "for the reception of public companies and societies." There was a coffeehouse on the first floor, and the space above could accommodate roughly three hundred people. In his diary, Durang suggests that he built a box, pit and gallery theater inside the building, as he had done in other locations while on tour.

CIRCUSES

Of course, Durang was not the first performer to present acts we would associate with a circus. There is a record of a touring performance in Baltimore in 1785 by Thomas Pool, who created what some consider to be "the first American circus" (although Pool did not use the word). He specialized in equestrian routines, such as riding two or three horses at top speed while standing and getting trained horses to perform tricks. Pool was known to finish his show with a version of *The Tailor's Ride to Brentford*, a sequence in which his horse would comically misbehave while he tried to mount it. This scene originated in England with legendary horseman Philip Astley, the man who created the prototype of the modern circus. "The Tailor's Ride" invoked the common cliché that tailors were poor horsemen with suspect masculinity. In one playbill, Pool advertised the bit as "The Taylor humourously riding to New York."

In the late 1790s, there were other circuses that visited Baltimore. Philip Lailson, a native of Sweden, led his company, the Equestrian Circus, to the city in 1798 and offered pantomime in addition to standard equine entertainment. He also may have used an innovation he introduced a year earlier, which later became common circus practice, a parade of costumed performers moving through the streets to drum up business.

The following year, John Bill Ricketts, the most influential circus performer to come to Baltimore, appeared. A dashing, highly skilled

Astley's Amphitheatre in London (1808), an example of a circus/theater combination. *Courtesy of the Metropolitan Museum of Art (Harris Brisbane Dick Fund, 1917).*

Englishman, he was a fixture in cities and towns throughout the East Coast, including Canada. Admired by George Washington, who rode with him occasionally, he was so popular that he built his own permanent circus in Philadelphia. In fact, when the Chestnut Street Theatre tried to hold performances on the same evening as Ricketts's circus, its business plummeted, and it was forced to go back to its original schedule. He even succeeded in making his horse Cornplanter a star.

By the time Ricketts played Baltimore, Durang had joined the company. He was utilized as a singer but was also featured in a pantomime called *Poor Jack or, The Sailor's Landlady*, in which he sang these lyrics as part of a catchy and patriotic drinking song:

> *When the full flowing bowl enlivens the soul,*
> *To foot it we merrily lead 'em;*
> *And each bonny lass will drink off her glass,*
> *To America, commerce, and freedom.*

Durang also danced the hornpipe, a mashup of ballet steps, traditional Scotch country dance, Irish footing and the shuffle-and-wing, a forerunner of modern tap dancing. In addition, he clearly had been taught horse comedy, because he was now entrusted to portray the hapless tailor with his horse.

Ricketts was not immune to bad fortune. In 1799, his Philadelphia building, the Pantheon (a popular name), caught fire and burned to the ground, the victim of a reckless carpenter who left a candle burning in scenery storage, where he "kept his bottle." With no insurance, Ricketts took a devastating loss of $20,000. Trying to get back on his feet but unable to pay a large company, he sent out a small touring group, but the dates in Georgetown, Alexandria and Annapolis were busts. Still, their luck changed in Baltimore, where they gave eighteen performances, a good run in those days. Those who attended saw most of Ricketts's classic feats, such as dancing on a saddle while his horse galloped at top speed and catching oranges with a fork. Ricketts charged white audience members one dollar for a seat in a box. Black audience members could pay half price but had to stand.[11]

It is likely that these circus tours used the Old American Company's former theater, which was known for many years as "the circus on Philpot's Hill." Durang's memoir specifically states that Ricketts's company performed "in

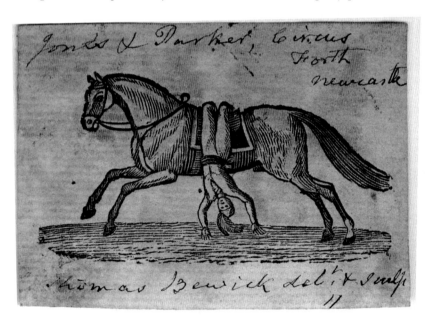

An acrobat performing *The Tailor's Ride to Brentford*; handbill and newspaper advertisement, 1790. © *The Trustees of the British Museum.*

a back street near the falls and middle bridge," which exactly describes the location of Hallam's theater. What is certain is that in 1811, a circus troupe headed by American Victor Pépin and Frenchman Jean Breschard came to Baltimore and took over the aging venue. They renamed it the Baltimore Olympic Circus and added the city to their touring schedule, which included Philadelphia, Boston, Charleston and Washington. The program was the same tried and true "Entertainment by Man and Horse" found in past circuses, but instead of a pantomime, they included a play entitled *Lovers' Vows*. This was an English adaptation of a German play called *Natural Son*, by August von Kotzebue, also mentioned in Jane Austen's novel *Mansfield Park* (1814). In the novel, the characters rehearse Kotzebue's play and then cancel their performance due to the play's inclusion of sex before marriage.

Ticket prices had not changed much in the intervening years—it was still a dollar for a box seat and half for the pit—but Pépin and Breschard still made a respectable $400 on their first night. Yet all were not pleased to see a play in a circus instead of a pantomime. One letter to a newspaper strongly complained:

> *I cannot help thinking, Mr. Editor, that this project of uniting theatrical with equestrian performances, may lead to the most dangerous perversion of an amusement, which, in its proper form, is both dignified and instructive.… The theatrical part of the establishment never can prove attractive, because the audience is from necessity so removed from the stage as to render it impossible, without a painful exertion, either to see or hear with tolerable distinctiveness.*

In 1818, the circus was separated from the presentation of plays not because of audience complaints but because of the expenses associated with the actors and scenery. Later, other management took over the site, and it remained a circus for some time.

WARREN AND WOOD'S NEW THEATRE

Thomas Wignell enjoyed his theatrical enterprise, which included the theater on Holliday Street, for roughly ten years. By 1803, he had stopped acting, instead devoting his time to management, and proposed marriage to the widowed English actress Anne Brunton Merry. She had been a great asset to the theater. When recruited by Wignell in 1796, she was already a veteran, having played fifty roles at two of London's major theaters by

MISS BRUNTON
in the Character of
HORATIA
In the Roman Father
"By this we'll swear a Lasting Love"
Act 3.ᵈ Scene 2.ᵈ

Anne Brunton Merry in her London debut, 1785. *From the University of Illinois Theatrical Print Collection.*

the age of twenty-seven. In her first marriage to Robert Merry, Anne had been the clear breadwinner. Robert was a poet and sometime playwright from a wealthy family. He had an earned reputation for laziness and had lost most of his fortune on gambling and an extravagant lifestyle. After he died in Baltimore in 1798, Anne mourned the loss, returned to the stage and continued to be very popular with American audiences. When she held a benefit at the Chestnut Street Theatre, her profits far outweighed those of others in the company. She was "praised for her sweet voice, gracefulness, and simplicity of manner," and one paper went as far as to describe her as "unquestionably the best serious actress that ever graced an American stage."

Anne's second marriage to Wignell was short-lived. He died weeks after they were married from an infection in his arm caused by a bloodletting procedure. Before his death, Anne had become pregnant, and she gave birth to a daughter in the fall of that year. Rather than be sidelined by motherhood, she signed a contract with Alexander Reinagle to comanage the Chestnut Street and Holliday Street Theatres for four years. This made her one of the first female theater managers in the country.[12] It was a difficult task to be sure. The duties of a nineteenth-century manager were extensive. In addition to acting if required, managers were responsible for choosing a season of plays, casting, directing actors, guiding scenic design, hiring and firing employees and handling finances, none of which were considered womanly pursuits at the time and are now handled by a variety of staff. Anne certainly had the knowledge. She grew up watching her father, an actor-manager in Norfolk, England, and as a performer, she was no stranger to the workings of professional theater. Although her fellow actors were said to be difficult, she comanaged the company until 1806. That year, she married a prominent comic actor in the company named William Warren and turned over her shares in the company to him. After Reinagle died, an actor and treasurer of the company, William Wood, bought equal shares and joined Warren as a comanager. Warren and Wood were to be the new theatrical power brokers of Philadelphia and Baltimore.

Of course, the art form still had its detractors. In 1812, a petition to ban theater was signed by 279 Baltimore citizens and sent to the mayor. It insisted that "All exhibitions of the theatre, circus and all others of like character" were "injurious to religion, morality, good order and life." The "threat to life" was a reference to a terrible fire that had broken out a month earlier at the Richmond Theatre in Virginia, where Alexandre Placide's company was playing. Before every performance, the chandelier over the audience was raised to indicate the start of the performance. Unfortunately, the candles set fire to the cords that lifted it, rapidly igniting the ceiling as well as the scenery on stage. While struggling to find an exit, seventy-two people were killed, and the grisly news sent shockwaves throughout the country. For the petition's signatories, those who died were not just victims of a poorly designed theater with inadequate exits. They were proof that theater was an immoral practice with mortal consequences. Thankfully, the petition had no effect.

Warren and Wood were optimistic about their prospects on Holliday Street and decided to tear down the wooden structure. They then built a brick theater in the same location. These were turbulent times in which to own a theater. Yellow fever was always a threat to financial survival, and tensions between Americans and the British had already erupted into the War of 1812. Baltimore, a busy port city, was a prime target. Only a week before the theater opened, a British raiding party destroyed some of the theater's scenery, which was being temporarily stored in a Havre de Grace warehouse. Painters had to be rushed from Philadelphia to finish the set so performances did not have to be canceled.

The New Theatre opened on May 10, 1813, featuring a play titled *The West Indian* (1771), a popular sentimental comedy about a mischievous plantation owner from the Caribbean who finds love in England. The 1,500-seat theater was still unfinished, so the audience had to be restricted to the lower boxes and the pit. After the theater's construction was completed the following year, one visitor described it as "not large, but well-arranged and tastefully decorated." An illustration shows a neoclassical façade and suggests a flight of stairs to an upper level, where the auditorium was located. It also contained a coffee room and boasted "a degree of accommodation not exceeded by any theatre in the United States." It was designed by Robert Carey Long Sr., who moved away from the Georgian style that had been imported from England. Long was later responsible for a host of other Baltimore landmarks. Four of them survive today (some in part): the University of Maryland School of Medicine, the Peale Museum, St. Paul's Episcopal Church and several row houses on Hamilton Street.

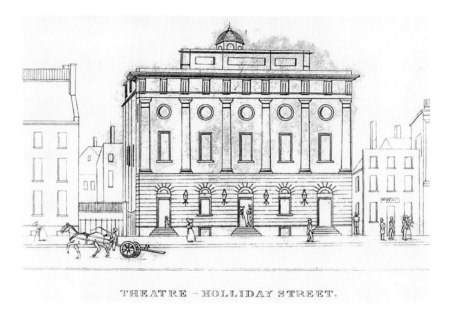

THEATRE - HOLLIDAY STREET.

The first Holliday Street Theatre. *From John H.B. Latrobe,* Picture of Baltimore *(Baltimore, MD: Fielding Lucas Jr., 1832), 189.*

By 1814, the war had reached Baltimore. After occupying and burning Washington, the British fleet menacingly entered Baltimore's harbor. With doom in the air, a crowd gathered on the roof of the theater to watch the bombardment of Fort McHenry. On one of the British ships was Francis Scott Key, who got trapped when he boarded the ship to arrange for the return of a prisoner of war. As he watched the attack, Key began to compose a poem describing the event and finished it when he was released. When the danger passed and the British retreated, Warren and Wood held a performance, with the profits going to "the fund for the defense of the city under the direction of the committee of vigilance and safety." At this benefit, Key's poem, now set to music by his brother-in-law and titled "The Star-Spangled Banner," was sung in public for the first time by an actor named Mr. Harding.

The song was only part of the theater's patriotic offerings. It was followed by another song called "The Patriotic Diggers," which gave the British this strong warning:

Enemies beware, keep a proper distance,
Else we'll make you stare at our firm resistance;
Let alone the lads who are freedom tasting,
Don't forget our dads gave you once a basting.

What came next was the unveiling of a painting that depicted the victory of the American navy over a far superior British fleet. This kind of programming was emblematic of this era of American theater, which was dominated by English actors and managers. Whether they were expressing genuine patriotism, outright pandering for box office gains or following a strategy to align themselves with American interests to mitigate their origins, the theaters' performances often included odes to figures such as George Washington or the singing of patriotic songs like "Hail Columbia." After the Revolution, the theater became a very public platform for American nationalism.

Although the environment was pro-American, the plays presented in Baltimore did not live up to the sentiments expressed in *The Contrast*, which suggested a new age of American voices on the stage. According to William Wood's account book, which covers twelve years, the company presented an astounding 379 different plays, operas, comic operas and pantomimes. Yet except for a handful of Shakespeare's plays, they were all pieces that were successful in London theaters, such as the Savoy, Haymarket and Covent Garden. Theatrically, Baltimore was still very much a British colony.

Determining the New Theatre's reputation is hard to establish, especially with the scarcity of available evidence. There were no established drama critics, and newspapers were paid to publish press releases, which were sometimes indistinguishable from reviews. Therefore, tales of delighted audiences should be looked at with a critical eye. Going by box office receipts is also difficult. Managers' complaints about remaining profitable have been true in every era, despite the quality of work, an occupational hazard in the arts. What is definitive is that some actors, admittedly a highly critical bunch, did not regard the work performed in the New Theatre very highly. For example, a British comedian named Joe Cowell, who toured extensively in the United States, wrote, "Baltimore had for years been visited by Warren and Wood, with the same jog-trot company and the same old pieces, till they had actually taught the audience to stay away."

The "Mud Theatre"

The plot of land that is now East Saratoga Street and Guilford Avenue was once known as the Pavilion Garden. This pleasure garden was owned by a John Finlay, described as "a rather eccentric chairmaker, but a well-meaning man."[13] The garden took its name from the structure at the center of the property, where entertainment was provided. Durang had performed at the Pavilion and sang its praises as "the best regulated garden in America." However, its location was in a low-lying part of the city known as the Meadows, which was prone to flooding and muddy streets. For example, in the same year Durang played, the Jones Falls River overflowed from the north and of the three wooden bridges traversing it, only the middle one survived. In fact, the damage to the garden was so extensive that Durang had to halt his performances for three weeks.

Perhaps Durang's presence prompted Finlay to dream bigger, because by the end of 1817, he and his two brothers had built a theater on his property and named it the Adelphi. Commonly called the "Mud Theatre," it was said that when the surrounding streets filled with water after a heavy rain, boats were needed to get patrons and employees to dry land. One late nineteenth-century historian called the Adelphi "a neat little structure, though not so elaborately ornamented as some of the dramatic establishments of the present day." Another far less charitable writer called it "a dingy little concern."

The location of the Adelphi highlights that even though theater was a popular pastime, it was not considered a product of high culture. The Meadows was not a reputable area. It was underdeveloped but still had its fair share of saloons, gambling houses and brothels whose business went unhindered by local authorities; it was not uncommon to find drunks and streetwalkers brawling in the streets. In the nineteenth century, the theater's role in the sex trade did not help its reputation. It was commonly assumed that sex workers displayed themselves in galleries to drum up business. Although there is evidence that this occurred, some scholars have questioned the extent of this practice. They assert that some accounts mislabeled working women as sex workers because they did not conform to expectations of what was considered "proper" attire and behavior. Unaccompanied women who did not attend the theater with a husband or family member were always sexually suspect.

The Adelphi's eight hundred seats were filled on its opening night. After a rousing overture and public address, the comedy *The Soldier's Daughter* (1804) was presented, as was the enduring comic opera *The Poor Soldier* (1783). By this time, *The Poor Soldier* was an old chestnut that revolves around Irish-born British soldiers returning to Ireland after fighting in the American Revolution. Believed to be a favorite of George Washington, it was very popular with American audiences ever since it was presented by the Old American Company in 1785. Although critics of this period found it to be past its prime, it remained a staple on the American stage until the Civil War. The opera might have owed its appeal to the universality of the poor common soldier, or audiences may have simply responded to the main characters' romantic struggles. In any case, the play is a good example of the Americanization of British material, a practice that could be contentious. For a New York production of *The Poor Soldier*, the lines for a comic French servant named Bagatelle were cut. This was an attempt to avoid criticism by those offended on behalf of America's French allies in the War of 1812. However, instead of stopping controversy, the change sparked a newspaper war about the censorship of ethnic portrayals in every city where the play was performed, an early debate about political correctness. It is unknown which version made it to the stage at the Adelphi Theatre, but when the opera was presented in Boston, Bagatelle was changed to Domingo, a Black servant, and no protest occurred. Shut out of the debate, Black citizens would have no forum or allies to criticize their portrayal on stage and could only watch from a special part of the gallery.

In the same year as its opening, the Adelphi boldly adopted gaslight, a new technology that would prove revolutionary to the theater and the world. In 1802, English geologist Benjamin Henfrey discovered a process that used coal gas to create what he called "inflammable air." He exhibited his creation in Baltimore when William Warren was in the city, but the municipal authorities were not impressed. Later, another researcher named Charles Kugler created another, more promising means of producing gas using tree resin. This innovation drew the interest of an idealistic artist named Rembrandt Peale, the son of Charles Willson Peale, who painted portraits of major colonial figures, such as Washington, Franklin, Hancock, Jefferson and Hamilton. The elder Peale was fascinated by natural history and was an avid collector of taxidermized American animals and birds, eventually installing his beloved collection into his passion project, the Philadelphia Museum.

The Adelphi Theatre. Its domed ceiling can be partially seen. *From John H.B. Latrobe,* Picture of Baltimore *(Baltimore, MD: Fielding Lucas Jr., 1832), 191.*

Rembrandt Peale, having the same interests as his father, opened the Peale Museum and Gallery of Painting in Baltimore in 1814. Located on Maryland and Holliday Streets, it was designed by Robert Carey Long Sr. and was the first building in America erected as a museum instead of occupying an existing space. But there was a problem. The museum was filled with treasures, such as the skeleton of a giant mastodon, bottles containing two-headed snakes and the younger Peale's own paintings, but they could be exhibited only in the daytime. To expand the museum's hours so it could make more money, Peale invited Kugler to put his theories into practice. In 1816, Kugler gave the museum its own gas plant.

Kugler's success at the museum led Peale, Long and others to fund the creation of the Gas-light Company of Baltimore on the corner of North and Saratoga Streets, directly across the street from the Adelphi. After the company got approval from the mayor and city council, it began to install pipes to light streetlamps and, initially, Baltimore's wealthier homes. Gas was installed in the Adelphi in 1817, making it the first public building in Baltimore and the second theater in the country to be lit by this new energy source.[14] Peale later claimed that he was defrauded out of his interest in the company. In 1822, he returned to painting and turned over the museum to his younger brother Rubens.

For the Adelphi and theaters everywhere, there were trade-offs to adopting gaslight. It was cheaper than candles and oil lamps, but repairs to pipes could be costly. Even though the auditoriums could not be darkened completely due to pilot lights, they could still be dimmed, which provided a greater sense of illusion and an increased sense of voyeurism. However, increased light on the stage could potentially have a negative impact on how actors were perceived. Declamatory acting executed in shadowy candlelight might have once seemed effective, but with brighter light, an actor's performance could now appear grotesque and their makeup garish. Gaslight's greater reach on the stage also meant that instead of crowding the stage's apron, looking for light, actors had to retreat behind the proscenium arch, which made the quality of the scenery more important than ever before.

Since there was concern that the fire in Richmond remained in the public's memory, the Adelphi's management advertised not only gaslight's aesthetic improvements but also its safety:

> *We may expect much novelty and look with some impatience for the production of the Melodrama of* Aladdin or The Wonderful Lamp....*The introduction of the Gas Lights, to the theatre, is an improvement which*

much instantly attract, by their transparent brilliancy the observation of the beholder, and are wonderfully calculated, by their easy management, in graduating light, to aid in the scenery requiring the necessary alterations in that respect. Their safety is also another strong recommendation and will serve to do away with those fears which sometimes interrupt the pleasures of the more timid part of the audience.

It is impossible to know if the theater managers recognized the irony of choosing a play about a magical oil lamp using a technology that made oil lamps obsolete. In any case, these comments underlined another major innovation in theatrical practice that was already in motion—the melodrama.

Early Melodrama

Melodramas were first performed in France after its bloody revolution and were aimed at working-class audiences, whose tastes were shifting away from simplistic pantomimes. Around 1800, they gained popularity in Europe and America and came to dominate nineteenth-century theater. *Melodrama* literally means "music drama" or "song drama." Its primary feature is music that is played to underscore spoken scenes in order to enhance their emotional value, a convention we take for granted in modern films. Of course, music was already an important part of theatrical evenings. It was played for patrons as they entered and during breaks in the program, and some early melodramas included interpolated songs, a prototype of the modern musical. Baltimore, in particular, benefitted from having the use of the Philadelphia orchestra, one of the largest in the country.

Melodramas were a natural extension of the eighteenth-century preoccupation with ethical behavior. They constructed an emotionally satisfying universe in which good always triumphs over evil. In every play, a virtuous hero or heroine is hounded by a villain but is always rewarded with a happy ending. Moral reversals are also possible. Sometimes, the villain is so impressed by the hero's virtue that he changes his ways in the final scene. Philosophically, melodramas conveyed the comforting notion that people are essentially good and that evil is not inherent but accidental.

William Wood's journal confirms melodrama's ascension. Between 1810 and 1823, only a handful of pantomimes were performed, while melodramas played a major part of every season. When looking at the titles chosen for the theater on Holliday Street, three themes emerge. The first were settings in exotic locales, coupled with a misunderstanding of non-Western cultures. Despite being set in Bagdad, George Coleman's *The Forty Thieves* (1799) included fairies, gnomes, sylphs and naiads, none of which existed in Middle Eastern mythology. The "Melo-Dramatic Romance" *Aladdin* was a mashup of Asian cultures: it was set in *Tartary*, a blanket term used by European cartographers to lump together China, parts of India, Persia and even Japan. Despite the play's suggestion of a Chinese locale, the characters had Muslim names.

The second theme was a sense of the gothic. *Blue Beard* (1798), another Colman play, was a French fairy tale relocated to Turkey. There, a violent bearded despot named Abomelique has married several times, but his wives have disappeared under mysterious circumstances. When his new bride, Fatima, comes to live in his castle, she is instructed to avoid one particular door. When she inevitably opens it, she finds a chamber that "exhibits various Tombs, in a sepulchral building;—in the midst of which ghastly and supernatural forms are seen;—some in motion, some fixed.—In the centre, is a large Skeleton, seated on a Tomb, (with a dart in his hand) and over his head, in characters of blood is written 'THE PUNISHMENT OF CUROSITY.'" When Abomelique tries to kill Fatima, the Skeleton becomes animated and intervenes. It plunges the dart into Abomelique's chest, and the two sink into the earth as "a volume of flame arises, and the earth closes," the most definitive ending for a villain you will ever find in a melodrama. The text is a classic example of the orientalist tradition, an outlook that portrays the East as a fantasyland filled with backward, barbaric and uncivilized people in need of positive Western influence.

Another example of gothic horror comes from James Robinson Planché's *The Vampire* (1820). It tells the story of Lord Ruthven, a nobleman who feeds on virgins. The play was a French melodrama given to Planché to adapt, but when he pointed out its historical inaccuracies, mainly its setting in Scotland, where no vampire lore existed, the manager of a London theater would not allow any changes to be made. He had his heart set on Scotch music and had the costumes in stock. The success of the production proved the manager was correct. English audiences (and, later, American ones) did not care about verisimilitude.

The third theme is what many called the sentimental "drama of situation," which prioritizes possibility over probability. In other words, convenient plot devices emerge to move the story forward, despite strained credibility. Examples popular in Baltimore were William Dimond's *The*

Foundling of the Forest (1809) and James Kenney's *The Blind Boy* (1808). Both are orphan stories that include the fortuitous discovery of noble parentage in the final scenes.

Another example is Kenney's *Ella Rosenberg* (1807), which played in the city for ten years.[15] The play consists of pathos and a series of happy accidents. In the first scene, the events of the past two years are revealed. Rosenberg, a young officer, used to be friends with the powerful and lustful Colonel Mountfort. Mountfort became obsessed with his wife, Ella, and, seeking to remove any obstacle, provoked Rosenberg to draw his sword and allowed himself to be wounded. Fearing military justice, Rosenberg fled to the capital in order to seek mercy from a more powerful nobleman, the Elector. Unfortunately, the Elector was surrounded by sycophants, who blocked Rosenberg from being heard. Rosenberg then went on the run, which led to his wealth being confiscated.

When the action of the play begins, Mountfort is now governor of the province, and Ella, poverty-stricken, is in hiding. Mountfort soon discovers her, and his confederates drag her away. After a series of coincidences and mortal threats, Ella, her husband and Mountfort all end up at the same house. Suddenly, the Elector enters and commutes Rosenberg's sentence; the wicked Mountfort is arrested, and with a flourish of drums and trumpets, the couple enjoy their newly found freedom. This type of deus ex machina resolution would be melodrama's stock in trade for a century. Like *The Vampire*, *Ella Rosenberg* also includes another of melodrama's most popular tropes: the defense of a woman's virtue against a cruel man with high status.

In these early melodramas, musical underscoring was not simply appended. It was written specifically for each show and was meant to be played at specific moments. In addition, playwrights were very explicit about the music's attributes. For example, in Thomas Holcroft's *A Tale of Mystery* (1802), he calls for music to express "discontent and alarm," "hunting," "chattering contention," "pain and disorder" and "confusion," all in the first scene. The music and the scenes were meant to have a symbiotic relationship, which is why the texts had great difficulty standing by themselves. For example, an 1808 review of *Ella Rosenberg* bluntly stated that "whatever interest may have been excited by this piece, when aided by music and adorned by the decorations of the theatre, we are obliged to say that, without these helps, it is flat and insipid."

The Front Street Theatre

The well-established Holliday Street Theatre eventually got bigger competition than the smaller Adelphi. The former home of the Old American Company had remained a circus, but now the structure was so decrepit that it was unusable. This prompted a group of local businessmen and tradesmen, including Thomas Wildy, the founder of the first Odd Fellows lodge, to make immediate plans to replace it by raising funds. They created a corporation called the Baltimore Theatre and Circus Company and imitated past schemes by selling $100 shares. As the group's name implies, it was intended for dramatic and equestrian performances.

Instead of rebuilding on the same site, it was decided that the theater should be located on the southwest corner of Front and Low Streets, with the Jones Falls at its back. Designed and built by Charles Grover, this four-story brick structure cost $27,000. Nineteenth-century historian John Thomas Scharf provided a very detailed description of the enormous space:

> The building is four stories high, has three tiers of boxes and a pit, and comfortably accommodates four thousand persons. There are three entrances on Front Street and one on Low....There were extensive dressing-rooms under the stage, and stabling for over fifty horses. In the rear of the stabling, bordering on the Falls, there was a spacious court with three large doors opening on the Falls, with steps descending to the water. The stage was seventy-five feet long and the same in breadth, with a large door twelve feet wide opening on the Falls, where a stage was erected over sixty feet long. The opening of the stage was thirty was thirty-four feet wide, with ways nine feet broad so as to admit horses or carriages. The ring was forty-seven feet in diameter, with two door, thirteen feet high and six feet wide, leading from the stables. The height from the dome to the ring was fifty-two feet; and the dressing-room was seventy feet long, twenty feet high, and the same in width. The scenery was perhaps the finest in the country.

The orchestra could seat forty or fifty musicians. The seats in the pit were designed to be easily removed for circus performances, and the entire building was lit with gas. There were three entrances on Front Street and a door on the side of the building used exclusively by Black audience members. Like the Holliday, this new theater was meant to be rented by touring companies. Dubbed the Theatre and Circus, it was the largest theater in America, a daring move, since there was doubt that Baltimore could support a venue of this size.

The Theatre and Circus, later the Front Street Theatre. *From George Washington Howard,* The Monumental City *(Baltimore, MD: J.D. Ehlers, 1873), 337.*

In June, the trustees advertised the theater's availability to any company that wished to occupy it. Four months later, it opened under the management of William Blanchard, who was responsible for successful circus tours in the United States and Canada. On the evening of September 10, 1829, an audience of roughly two thousand watched as an actress named Mrs. Hill delivered a lengthy opening-night poem. It included a passage that spoke to the theater's utility as an arena for teaching morality:

> *Beauty and youth shall oft assemble here,*
> *And the bright eye be dimm'd with many a tear!*
> *The Virgin's heart shall shrink, her cheek grow pale,*
> *As sorrow here unfolds its piteous tale;*
> *But Virtue still shall triumph, Vice despair,*
> *As godlike Justice drags it from its lair!*

Blanchard's company played for an impressive two hundred nights. One of the pieces he chose to perform was seemingly custom-made for the Theatre and Circus, Matthew Lewis's *Timour the Tartar* (1811). This English work was one of the first written to include live horses instead of adding them to an existing play in production. This genre came to be known as hippodrama, or the more colloquial "horse drama." Its origin is a testimony to theatrical ingenuity. In England, Philip Astley wanted to stage dramatic plays in addition to circus acts but was restricted due to the Licensing Act of 1737, the same legislation that brought the Hallams to America. But Astley found a loophole. Traditional plays could be presented, provided the performers were, for the most part, on horseback. The plays Astley "mounted" were very successful and got mainstream theaters wanting to cash in. Soon, Covent Garden remounted Coleman's *Blue Beard* as a hippodrama, using twenty of Astley's trained horses. That production's enormous success led them to produce *Timour the Tartar*, a money-maker that ended up living on stages in England and the United States for the next fifty years.

The plot is a setup for pure spectacle. The cruel Timour, a man of humble origins, has killed a prince of Mingrelia and now holds the prince's heir in his dungeon. The prince's widow, Zorilda, tries to rescue the young prince, but she is discovered and imprisoned. The prince escapes and joins a group of Georgian warriors who attack Timour's fortress and free the princess. The printed text is filled with processions ("the horses withdraw, after paying their homage to Timour") and military combat ("enter on horseback—they charge with lances"). In the end, it is a horse that heroically resolves the action. During the final battle scene, the prince "leaps his horse over the parapet" and disappears into a pool of water where Zorilda is drowning. All seems lost until the horse heroically reemerges from the water with the two of them on its back.

The Theatre and Circus's season ran from September 1 until July 4. There is a mention of a company run by a Mr. Willis playing throughout 1830, but rental advertisements that follow suggest that keeping the theater occupied for the entire season was difficult, especially when a wave of cholera entered the city. To drum up business, John Lamb, the theater's manager at the time, held a contest for the best-written equestrian melodrama in 1831. The prize was $100 and part of one night's receipts, but the winner, if there was one, is unknown. The following year, a raffle was introduced with prizes, including a writing desk, a lady's toilet, fashionable boots, a snuffbox and a cow.

As to be expected, there was fierce competition between the city's two major theaters, and class distinctions played a part. The Holliday Street Theatre was in a fashionable area and drew more upper-class clientele, while the Theatre and Circus charged less and catered more to the middle and poorer working classes. Once these reputations were established, major stars gravitated to the Holliday. Additionally, there was a clear bias in the coverage by local newspapers, which mentioned every major engagement at the Holliday, while the Theatre and Circus was mostly ignored. What did make it into print was the animosity between the two theaters. It started when the manager of the Holliday Street accused Lamb of using a version of the opera *Cinderella* that he had already contracted from New York's Park Theatre. Lamb responded by dismissing the accusation and fanning the flames of class warfare. He proudly stated to the press: "If I produce any drama I am answerable to my audience, and not to the people of the Holliday Street Theatre, or any one connected with its government, but to avoid mistakes [on their part] for the future I shall designate my house as the People's Circus and Theatre." In the same spirit, Tyrone Power, a popular Irish actor who appeared several times on Front Street, wrote in his book, "I have discovered that the people are with us. The Holliday being considered the aristocratic house, and the Front, being, indeed, the work of an opposition, composed of the sturdy democracy of our good city." In 1832, the strife between the two theaters was quelled somewhat when the Holliday Street managers leased the Front Street Theatre for the next five years.[16]

The "sturdy democracy" Power mentioned was not extended to everyone at the Theatre and Circus. For white audiences, boxes cost fifty cents, and the pit cost twenty-five cents. Black audiences also paid twenty-five cents but were forced to sit in a designated section of the gallery. Although the racial segregation of neighborhoods was not common in Baltimore, the segregation of theater audiences remained standard practice well into the twentieth century. Even the enjoyment of Black patrons irked some white audience members. One pleaded to a local paper, "Could not the notes of the Ethiopians in the gallery be somewhat allayed; they are truly annoying."[17]

On November 15, 1837, local competition seemed to intensify with the opening of the Olympic Circus on Pratt Street. Formerly a building known as the Repository, its shares were sold to fund its transformation into a theater. A reporter was given a tour of the eight-hundred-seat theater, and he could not contain his excitement when he beheld the interior: "On ascending the flight of steps that conducted me to the Boxes, the view that met my eye seemed as 'twere a magical illusion. Never had I witnessed a greater display of taste in fitting up a place of amusement." He also wrote that the theater had a dome with "a splendid chandelier" and was "brilliantly lighted with gas."

The first tenant was circus manager Charles H. Bacon. In an attempt to indicate a family-friendly atmosphere, Bacon sent coded messages through his advertising. First, no ladies would be admitted "unless accompanied by Gentlemen," reassuring the public that there would be no sex workers in their gallery. Second, Bacon also ensured that "efficient Police will be in attendance to ensure good order," meaning that rowdy audiences would be controlled. Although the comfortable interior of the theater may have been surprising, Bacon's program was nothing new; in addition to feats of horsemanship, gymnastics, singing and dancing, a pantomime was presented as an afterpiece. After Bacon moved on, the theater was occupied by Howe's Olympic Circus, but there is only one other record of the space being used: a concert of sacred music given by the members of the Colored Musical Association. It is impossible to imagine how they felt entering and exiting the venue. Across the street, there was a slave market that included a private jail that could be rented to slave owners. In 1844, an advertisement seeking to rent the space appeared, but then the Olympic Circus seemingly disappears from history.

THE "MUSEUMS"

After a long struggle to remain open, the Peale Museum was lost to creditors and sold at public auction. It was purchased by the mayor and city council and repurposed as the new city hall. By January 1830, all of the museum's exhibits and paintings were, according to Peale, transferred to "a splendid building lately erected expressly for this establishment at the corner of Calvert and Baltimore streets." It was built by John Clark, a financial broker, who rented the upper floors to Peale and used the bottom floor to sell state lottery tickets. The location seemed ideal, as it was a busy promenade used for selling dry goods, and there were many fancy stores that catered to Baltimore's wealthier citizens.

Peale's Museum, as it was initially called, could best be described as a "dime museum," even though the admission price was usually twenty-five cents. Unlike European museums, which were owned by wealthy citizens, libraries or scientific societies, museums in America could not rely on philanthropy to keep the lights on. In Peale's case, he had five stockholders who had to see an 8 percent return on their investment, so he had to depend on showmanship to stay afloat. To drive ticket sales, many items were displayed more for their novelty than scientific relevance (like George Washington's shaving brush), and many live exhibitions were booked primarily for their sensational appeal. The offerings shown in Peale's "lecture room" included

The Baltimore Museum, 1850. Market Street (now Baltimore Street), looking west from Calvert. *Courtesy Enoch Pratt Free Library, Maryland's State Library Resource Center.*

plays, bands, ventriloquists, a "splendid Grotto Scene taken from *Cinderella*" and a mechanical reproduction of a bomb exploding under the palace of the Kremlin. Demonstrations were often pseudoscientific. One presenter encouraged an audience member to bring a gun, load it in full view and fire it at his chest. Another described himself as a professor of chemistry and the "Pyrotechnic Arts." He put a live rabbit into an oven and allowed it to die, then immediately exposed a dog to the same heat and claimed to rescue it with his special antidote. Afterward, the "professor" swallowed phosphorus and inhaled arsenic vapor but avoided a fatal end by drinking the same miraculous formula.

In 1834, Edmund Peale, Rubens's nephew, assumed full management. He renamed the venue the Baltimore Museum and Gallery of Fine Arts and decided to convert its lecture room into a theatre. It was reported to have had three tiers of box seats, but there is only one mention of its overall size. A visitor to the city was taken by friends to see a play and described the theater as "about the size off a six-stalled stable, and full of rowdies, etc.— no ladies." The museum would occasionally advertise its plays' educational value, but essentially, the theater served as one of the city's main theatrical venues. Later, the exhibits were removed and only the theater remained, but it retained its name. *Museum* continued to be a very flexible word.

The museum's saloon was said to fit five hundred people. In 1845, an item in the paper mentions a performer playing multiple engagements at the saloon, a place to "pass an evening in innocent mirth and rational enjoyment." This means that either the saloon had some kind of raised stage

A New York concert saloon. *From* Harper's Weekly *3, no. 145 (October 8, 1859): 641.*

for performers, or the section of the theater that we now call the orchestra was filled with tables and chairs for drinkers. If the latter is true, the museum may have been an early "concert saloon," giving opponents of both alcohol and theater much cause for complaint, especially when these venues became more popular (and notorious) in the 1860 and 1870s.

Around the time Peale's original museum was being sold, a rival appeared in the city called the Washington Museum. Operating roughly from 1829 to 1849, it boasted an ample collection of wax figures, paintings, birds, reptiles and other animals. Until 1843, it was located on East Baltimore Street near South Street and then moved to the corner of Pratt and Mill Streets (near the bridge). Like Peale's Museum, the Washington Museum not only featured curiosities such as orangutans, a three-horned ox, a thirty-seven-inch-tall dwarf and an "electrifying machine," but it also hired acts such as minstrel performers, a marionette theater and a plate waltzer (one who spins plates on a long table). In 1844, it briefly installed a company of nine performers to perform dramas, comedies and farces. The number of seats in the performance space is unknown, but the museum boasted that its saloon could accommodate five hundred, so it may also have been a form of concert saloon. Tickets cost twelve and a half cents and came with an admission policy worth mentioning. Black audience members were allowed entry only during the day, which excluded them from all evening performances. This earned the museum the distinction of being the most segregated theater space in Baltimore.

Information about the Washington Museum is spotty. It goes unmentioned in the city's histories, and despite its longevity, it never became a significant touring stop for professional actors. Not much is known about its proprietors, except that a man named John P. Paul opened the museum with one of Rubens Peale's former assistants and ran it for over ten years. Paul came to a sad end in 1850. He left his residence in an altered mental state, talking continuously about money. Two weeks later, it was discovered that he had changed into old clothes in the woods and walked to the city; he was soon found dead on the street. It is hard not to wonder if his destination was the shuttered museum.

THE ASCENDANCY OF JIM CROW

By the time Thomas Dartmouth Rice ("T.D." or "Daddy" Rice) got to Baltimore in November 1837, he was in high demand. He played for three nights at the Holliday Street Theatre and then immediately appeared at the Front Street for four with his "highly and justly celebrated representative of negro characters." Rice had just returned from a successful yearlong tour of England, Scotland and Ireland that had solidified his status as the first American international superstar. Of course, blackface performance was nothing new. Many English plays brought to the United States had African and West Indian servant characters played by white actors. However, Rice's success in putting racial impersonation center stage forever changed the course of American theater while tapping into cultural ideas about race so complex that we are still debating them today.

Rice was born in New York in 1808, and like most of the northern performers who would eventually impersonate Black southern characters, he grew up with little to no contact with southern culture or slavery. Born into a poor family, he lived in the Seventh Ward along the East River, an ethnically diverse working-class neighborhood. He apprenticed for a carpenter who carved figureheads for ships, but by the 1820s, he seemed to have abandoned that trade and was trying his hand at acting. He performed in small roles in New York theaters, including the Park, which fired him for trying to steal scenes by drawing focus. By 1828, Rice had somehow found his way into a troupe run by Samuel Drake, who played Kentucky and other frontier areas. Still a novice, Rice did bit parts and created props as needed; nothing seemed to point to a profitable career. However, when playing in Louisville, Rice claimed to have repeatedly seen and heard a crippled stable hand singing and dancing to a lively tune outside his window. Inspired, Rice had the man teach it to him. Other accounts say Rice paid the stable hand and bought his clothes to use as a costume. In any case, Rice convinced Drake to let him perform the song between the acts of a serious play. This is how the soon-to-be iconic song began:

> *Come listen all you galls and boys*
> *I's jist from Tuckyhoe*
> *I'm goin to sing a little song,*
> *My name is Jim Crow.*
> ---
> *Weel about and turn about and do jis so,*
> *Eb'ry time I weel about and jump Jim Crow.*

Rice's delivery, along with his syncopated dancing, caused Louisville audiences to go "wild with delight," and at one performance, he received twenty curtain calls. All at once, Rice had a trademark character and a career. By the time he toured abroad, he had inspired a craze for his comic conception of Blackness. "In London," wrote the *Spirit of the Times*, "Jim Crow is even more popular than in New York. It is heard in every circle, from the soirées of the nobility, to the hovels of the street sweepers. 'Tis Jim Crow here—Jim Crow there—Jim Crow every where."

Noah Ludlow, a theater manager who worked with Rice, remembered him as a gifted mimic and recounted a story where he deftly imitated other actors in the company, a skill, he wrote, that he successfully applied to the "genuine corn-field negro, drawn from real life." This is indicative of numerous affectionate comments about Rice's work, suggesting an almost surgical accuracy in his imitation. Although today we find blackface performance to be a forum for hurtful caricatures, whether intentional or not, white America believed—or wanted to believe—in the authenticity of Rice's performance.

What complicates the Jim Crow narrative is that Rice's character was not just a lazy factotum. He was a kind of trickster hero, a lord of misrule and a disruptor of social mores. The audience was encouraged to laugh at him, but his character claimed high status not just for himself but for other Black people. These verses were part of his signature song:

No my brodder ni**ers
I do not think it right,
Dat you should laugh at dem
Who happen to be white.

Kase it dar misfortune,
And dey'd spend ebery dollar,
If dey only could be
Gentlemen ob colour

It almost break my heart,
To see dem envy me,
An from my soul I wish dem,
Full as black as we.

Here, there is an acknowledgment that derision based on feelings of superiority toward Black people was also mixed with fascination. For many white people, blackface minstrelsy was a window through which to observe what they thought was Black culture, despite its warped presentation.

Rice had been to the Front Street back in 1832. He had been hired for a few nights to do his comic Jim Crow song between plays performed by big-name actors. However, by 1837, he was no longer a novelty act. He was now a headliner and arrived with several vehicles created for his English tour. The result was a strange union of English playwriting and the jarring appearance of Rice's American blackface characters. At the Holliday, Rice presented *Jim Crow in London* (1837), a rewrite of William Concrieff's *Tom and Jerry in London* (1823). He also appeared in *The Virginia Mummy*, an adaptation of William Bayle Bernard's *The Mummy* (1833), in which he played Ginger Blue, a Black hotel waiter. At the Front Street, he performed in *The Peacock & The Crow* (1837), a farce written for Rice by Tom Parry in which Jim Crow was a saucy bootblack. Rice also appeared in another farce entitled *Black and White; or, the Mysterious Statues*, in which he portrayed Sambo, a dimwitted servant character. Almost all the appearances of Rice's characters read like interpolations. His characters do not serve the plot in any crucial way, and their function seems to be an opportunity for Rice to deliver quips and malapropisms in a tortured dialect.

The most American contribution to Rice's Front Street engagement was the one-act musical extravaganza he created called *Bone Squash Diavalo* (1835). This "Ethiopian opera" was set in Five Points, a notorious slum in lower

T.D. Rice in his Jim Crow costume. *From the Library of Congress, Prints and Photographs Division, LC-DIG-pga-13926.*

Manhattan where many free Black people resided next to Irish immigrants.[18] After a streetcorner scene in which Bone Squash, a chimney sweep, trades barbs with other blackface characters, Sam Switchell, the white Yankee Devil, appears. Sam convinces Bone to sell his soul to become an upper-class gentleman. Now in spiffy new clothes, Bone goes to romance two ladies, but the play immediately devolves into an extended chase scene in which the devil tries and fails to claim Bone. In the end, the devil tries to put Bone into a balloon to take him away. Bone cuts him loose, and the devil falls to the ground, where he gets swallowed back to hell. The play ends with Bone ascending in the same balloon as fireworks fill the stage.

Rice was described by his contemporaries as a tall "scrambling-looking fellow with a sepulchral falsetto voice." Walter M. Leman, an actor who played with Rice, called him a "genial, well-informed gentleman, with a most affable temper, which made him a charming companion." Rice was also known to be eccentric. He had a wooden statue of himself as Jim Crow created, and it was placed in front of theaters in New York where he was playing. After his London tour, he was known to wear a blue dress coat with buttons made of five- and ten-dollar gold pieces that he would rip off and give away to fans as souvenirs. This cavalier attitude regarding money did not serve him later in life. He squandered his fortune and turned to drink after an illness. Funds had to be raised to give him a proper burial after his death.

Rice's legacy is complex, especially considering this period of history. His meteoritic rise came during a time when the institution of slavery was beginning to be questioned, but there was immediate pushback from anti-abolitionists that led to riots in northern cities like Philadelphia, Utica and New York's Five Points. Although there were plenty of free Black people and even Black churches in Baltimore, the city remained the main port for the selling and shipping of enslaved people to New Orleans. Every newspaper contained rewards for the return of runaways who sought to be free of slavery's cruelty and degradation. In some ways, the figure of Jim Crow sat in the center of these opposing forces. He was both a sympathetic figure and a buffoon deserving of mockery.

This balance would soon change. In the 1840s, Rice's imitators would create a new kind of entertainment called the minstrel show, a type of blackface performance with the following set format. A group of performers would parade into a semicircle. The interlocutor or master of ceremonies would then trade jokes with the men on either end. On one side was Mr. Tambo, who played the tambourine, and on the other was Mr. Bones, who musically rattled sticks. Songs followed, a medley of specialty acts, and sometimes, the show would end with a short comic play or musical, a parody of a serious Shakespearean play or opera. Minstrelsy would have the dubious distinction of being the only form of theater invented in the United States.

Although Rice's Jim Crow was a grotesque distortion, the character had some agency, and his "Jump, Jim Crow" song was, at the very least, a product of Black culture. However, over time, minstrel show portrayals of Black characters got progressively more retrograde, and the music used, despite claims of representing genuine plantation life, were simply popular songs written by white composers like Stephen Foster. Moreover, minstrel shows took various blackface creations and fused them together. Jim Crow might exist side by side with Sambo or Zip Coon, a free urban dandy who "put on airs," along with characters from *Uncle Tom's Cabin*. Even after the Union victory, the minstrel show would retain its popularity for the next fifty years in both the North and the South.

After Rice appeared, the next resident at the Theatre and Circus on Front Street was Cooke's Equestrian Circus. Thomas Taplin Cooke—rider, rope walker and strong man—was part of an English circus family who had been in operation since 1752. After he took over the company from his father, he traveled to New York in three sailing ships with 130 people, including 37 family members. They played to some success and traveled to Boston. Then in Philadelphia, Cooke built a stone and brick amphitheater for 2,000 people when no venue could be secured (this was before the common practice of exclusively using tents). When that run was completed, Cooke took his company to Baltimore and played at the Theatre and Circus for six weeks.[19]

On February 3, 1838, between four and five o'clock in the morning, a fire was discovered, and bystanders saw flames pouring out of every door and window. It might have been controlled, but firefighters could not set up their engines. The front wall was too unstable and toppled into the street. In twelve hours, the entire theater was gone, as was an adjacent tavern. Cooke lost all of his stock scenery, costumes and machinery, but what was most horrifying was that his entire stud of fifty horses, full-blooded Arabian and Burmese ponies, had been stabled beneath the stage and had no way to escape.

There was one theory about the fire's cause. The previous night, the company had presented Henry M. Milner's *Mazeppa or The Wild Horse of Tartary* (1831), a drama famous for the scene in which a young man is lashed to a wild horse so he can be galloped to death. It was reported that the fireworks used in the show had ignited the scenery. The fire was

The burning of the Front Street Theatre and Circus. *From Mitchell Gold, "The Front Street Theatre (From Its Beginning to 1838)," master's thesis, Johns Hopkins University, 1948.*

immediately put out by stagehands, but it was thought that smoldering embers took over in the night.

Cooke was not insured, and his losses were estimated at $42,000. Immediately, there was an outpouring of sympathy and offers of assistance. Locals held a meeting and passed a resolution "to open books of subscriptions on his behalf" and to hold a benefit for him at the Holliday Street Theatre. Many offered to give him horses, but there was no replacement for years of training. Ultimately, these kind gestures did not change his bitterness about his experience in America. After a subsequent failed run in Philadelphia, he returned to England—but not before he claimed that he had been burned out due to jealousy.

The fire on Front Street did not destroy local enthusiasm for the theater. Immediately, new stock was issued to raise funds, and the theater was rebuilt before the end of the year. An English carpenter turned architect named William Minifie designed and erected a new theater with an austere neoclassical façade. Advertisements soon appeared for what was called the New Amphitheatre (later the American Amphitheatre), announcing that it would reopen on December 3, 1838, under the management of Francis Wemyss.

"THE WORST THEATRICAL TOWN IN AMERICA"

Francis Courtney Wemyss had a lengthy career. He was born in Boston but was educated in Scotland after the death of his father. At sixteen, he entered a lucrative but joyless business with his uncle. While visiting his mother in London, he fell into company with Scottish actor Henry Johnston (fresh from debtors' prison), who fanned his love of theater. Sometime later, Wemyss refused to copy a letter for his uncle after business hours, and in a fit of anger, his uncle struck him. Later, Wemyss would write that this blow transformed him into an actor. With new resolve, he walked thirty-six miles to join Johnston's company in Edinburgh. Johnston could not persuade him to abandon this course of action, and so began a lifelong profession.

Over time, Wemyss traveled with other theater companies in Scotland and England, learning from the greatest actors of the day. He came to America in 1822 for an engagement in Warren and Wood's Chestnut Street Theatre in Philadelphia. For one season, Wemyss acted at the Holliday Street Theatre, where low receipts meant actors had to settle for two-thirds of their contract wages. A good night in Philadelphia would gross over $800. In Baltimore, they were lucky to get over $200. Wemyss called this lackluster box office "no uncommon occurrence." In fact, his autobiography makes a point of calling out Baltimore for its miserable audiences throughout the 1820s. He wrote that the Holliday was "decidedly one of the prettiest but worst attended theatres in the United States" and proclaimed Baltimore to be "the worst theatrical town in America."

From the beginning, Wemyss and manager William Wood had a persistent dislike for each other, which led to a petty and public feud. While playing an English adventurer, Wemyss spoke the following line during a rehearsal: "When my fortunes shall be inquired after, my friend, with joy sparkling through a tear, may say, 'Herbert stuck to his commander to the last, and died as every Englishman should.'" Wood insisted he substitute "brave man" for "Englishman." Wemyss felt offended by the prejudice against his countrymen and asked the reason for the change. Wood replied that the necessity was "his will and pleasure," and an ugly scene

Francis Courtney Wemyss in a comedy called *The Honey Moon*, 1826. *From the University of Illinois Theatrical Print Collection.*

followed. Later, Wemyss got word that a party was being formed to hiss at him during a performance, and he suspected Wood's influence. When the evening came, Wemyss defiantly spoke the original line and was greeted with displeasure from the audience. He responded by stopping the play and pleading his case. Just when he seemed to be winning the audience to his side, Wood, who was also acting in the show, appeared on stage alongside him and condemned his actions to the audience. As the two men argued, the audience became impatient and insisted they go on with the play. In the end, Wemyss may have come out on top, for he had the good fortune of returning to this line: "I have not had a bit of fighting for a long time, and damn, if this has not given me a relish for it." This generated much laughter, and when Wood reentered the scene in character, he became the one harangued with hissing. After the incident, the two did not exchange words offstage for the next four years.

After Wemyss came into some money, he went into business with a Baltimore lottery and exchange broker and made more than he ever had as an actor. When Wood retired from management in 1827, Warren offered Wemyss the management of the Chestnut Street Theatre in Philadelphia and the Holliday Street Theatre in Baltimore. He jettisoned his lottery business and was soon tasked with going to England to recruit more actors. By this time, there was great competition for talent from the Park and Bowery Theatres in New York, the Tremont Theatre in Boston and the Walnut Street Theatre, their direct competitor in Philadelphia. Being an actor in America no longer had the reputation of a dangerous frontier adventure, and dozens of British actors contacted Wemyss, looking for employment. At the time he hired his company, the average contract was three or four dollars per week, but the more esteemed actors could get upward of twenty-seven.

As a manager, Wemyss had to walk a fine line with his audiences, who were extremely thin-skinned about any perceived slight aimed at the United States. When a rumor circulated that he had forbidden the orchestra in Philadelphia to play the "national airs, nightly called for by the audience," he immediately inserted a promise into the playbill that any requested songs would be played. This directive exasperated the leader of his orchestra, who had to jettison Mozart and others for "the frequent repetition of 'Yankee Doodle.'" Later, Wemyss tried to put the matter of national allegiance to rest with the renovation of his Philadelphia theater. Each tier of boxes was decorated with paintings of celebrated American battle scenes, the second and third tier of boxes were adorned with the likenesses of American generals and naval heroes and the dress circle had medallions of the heads of presidents. However, this cosmetic change would not please all parties. One socialite wrote on the back of a theater bill that Wemyss was "an Englishman who hates everything American, and yet puffs his theatre as the *Patriotic* House of the City."

Relations between Wemyss's theaters and the press were also strained. Wemyss had a litany of complaints. Back then, actors could pay newspapers to print "puff communications," a flattering account of their performance which, to the uninitiated, seemed identical to reviews by staff writers. "For a few dollars," wrote Wemyss, an actor "can have his own opinion of his abilities paraded in the newspapers, to procure fame at a distance from the circle where his merit is known and classed." Wemyss even alluded to blackmail, suggesting that newspapers extorted money from actors who did not want a bad review. The free tickets Wemyss had to dole out also made him bristle. Editors demanded them, according to Wemyss, in spite of their "unprovoked abuse and hostility towards the theatre where he was an invited guest." Sometimes, advertising was denied until tickets were given.

Baltimore remained a thorn in Wemyss's side. He called the 1828 season at the Holliday a failure and blamed the theater's 126 stockholders who, instead of releasing their free box seats when they could not attend, sold them for twenty-five cents. Like most theater managers, he acutely felt the economic recession of the following year (caused by a yearlong British ban on American trade). By 1830, he had abandoned both theaters, reopened his lottery business and returned exclusively to acting for a time. But Wemyss could not stay away. After a stint creating a theater in Pittsburgh, he decided to return to Philadelphia in 1834 and leased the same two theaters he had managed years before. By 1838, he had also become the manager of the Front Street Theatre, where the following episode took place. At a production of *Jane Shore* (1714), a play about the accomplished mistress of Edward IV, the actress playing the titular character lay down to die, but suddenly, a weather-beaten sailor rushed to the stage and insisted she take money from him so she could buy food. After a brief explanation, he was conducted back to his seat while the audience cheered him.

In 1841, Wemyss's career as a manager came to an end. While attempting to open the Arch Street Theatre in Philadelphia, he ran into trouble when promised gas fixtures were not ready, and the season had to be abandoned. In Baltimore, his luck was not much better, as the massive political rallies for William Henry Harrison and Martin Van Buren had drained the public's desire for theatricals. When he returned to Philadelphia, he reopened the Arch Street, but his lead actor could not stay sober for the run.[20] Receipts plummeted, and Wemyss's funds were completely drained. He was arrested for his debts, and to stay out of prison, all of his interests were sold. In the end, he moved to New York and became an actor again, ending twenty years of trying to gauge what audiences wanted to see. In the last years of his life, he worked in the box office at the Bowery Theatre, writing a history about the past one hundred years of the American stage.

Wemyss was a manager in a time when life became even more complicated for actors. In the past, they had been part of stock companies, groups of players who were chosen to perform a season of plays. When it became increasingly obvious to American managers that the glamour of a celebrity would boost sales, they tempted successful English actors to travel to the states for high salaries. This was the beginning of what was called the "star system," a practice that managers like William Wood believed had a corrosive effect. Celebrities were not dependent on the success of the box office, so they could force concessions such as half or all of an evening's receipts, as well as a clear benefit. This increase in the number of benefits devoted to stars meant there were fewer for company members. At the same time, managers offset the cost of stars by paying some actors by the show instead of contracting them for an entire season. This meant that many actors were forced to knit together a patchwork of dates in different theaters in order to earn a living. Soon, American actors realized that the best way to be financially successful was to become stars themselves, a difficult path in an industry dominated by overseas talent.

3

ACTORS, MOBTOWN AND THE CIVIL WAR

The first half of the nineteenth century was not an era of excellent plays. Rarely are any revived. It was, however, a time of great performances; the Holliday, Adelphi and Front Street Theatres hosted a generation of distinguished actors. Although it is impossible to be exhaustive in a study of this size, it would be a terrible omission not to highlight some of the colorful stars who "trod the boards."

EARLY ENGLISH CELEBRITIES

One of the earliest, most notable English players to perform in Baltimore was James Fennell. He was from a wealthy family and was described as a tall, remarkably handsome man. At Trinity College, he made some effort to study law but loved to gamble at cards—what he later called "a detestable and dishonourable practice"—and periodically racked up substantial debts. Even though he had very little experience performing in college, Fennell suddenly decided to become an actor, and in 1787, he confidently traveled to Edinburgh to start this new profession. After spending a period as an amateur, he became an audience favorite and played theaters in and around London. He spent his money freely, which forced his father to help him financially, but he was disowned by other members of his family not for his debts but for the inexcusable crime of becoming an actor. Fennell always had a restless mind—what he called "the eccentricity of my disposition." His life was filled

James Fennell. *From the University of Illinois Theatrical Print Collection.*

with unfinished projects, such as various encyclopedias, a treatise on wheat and the translation of an opera. He even claimed to have briefly studied electricity, which he used to restore a child's use of both their legs and an arm. His personal life seemed to have the same impulsiveness. At one point, Fennell fell "violently in love" with Anne Brunton Merry, but, unable to speak of his feelings, he was obliged "to sigh in secret" and give his "breathings to the passing winds."

In 1793, he accepted Thomas Wignell's offer of employment and boarded a ship to America with other Wignell draftees, such as William Warren. Twenty-nine days later, Fennell arrived in New York and made his way to Philadelphia but found the city in the clutches of yellow fever; the entire company had to flee to "the Jerseys" for three weeks, where they lived with various farmers. When the danger passed, they played in Annapolis, where Fennell played Othello in blackface. At one performance, "a country gentleman in the boxes" was so impressed by the intelligence of the titular character that he inquired after the show if his master would sell him for $500. Fennell would go on to play a variety of Shakespearean characters, including Hamlet, Macbeth and Hotspur. In doing so, he played a part in raising Shakespeare's reputation in America by luring many to the playhouse who had only experienced him in print. While in Baltimore, Fennell played the Holliday Street Theatre, and for a brief time, the Baltimore Olympic Circus.

Over the years, Fennell attempted several business schemes, but none were successful. He abruptly left the theater for a time to start an enterprise in Baltimore that would extract salt from seawater, but it fell apart. He also tried to run a boys' school of "Reading and Elocution" in Philadelphia, supported by a group of Quakers. However, they promptly deserted him when he had two young women act in scenes with him for a demonstration. Between occupations, Fennell's funds were sometimes so low that he would take work as a laborer to make ends meet. In his memoir, Fennell mentions a Baltimore man who gave him free lodging for sixteen months when he was broke. One biographer wrote that he never paid his bills and "passed his life between a palace and a prison," a reference to his being jailed for his debts in Baltimore and elsewhere. He returned to play at various theaters periodically but could never settle into a permanent situation.

Another popular actor recruited by Wignell was Thomas Abthorpe Cooper. Born into a London middle-class home, he was the son of a surgeon posted in India. When his father died, the family was so destitute that his mother took a position as a housekeeper, and her three boys were sent to live with relatives. Eleven-year-old Thomas Cooper went to live with his cousin William Godwin, a former minister who had traded his religious beliefs for liberal ones. The two had a contentious relationship, but Godwin shared his love of theater with Cooper and even read all of Shakespeare's plays to him. At fifteen, the excitable young man shocked his adoptive father by proclaiming that he was going to walk to Paris to join the republican army. Godwin managed to hold off the boy's ambitions by suggesting he take up the stage. He had a playwright friend coach the young man and give him a letter of introduction for the manager of the Edinburgh Theatre. In 1792, like Fennell before him, Cooper set off to Scotland to start a new life.

Cooper immediately found himself at odds with the acting style of the day, which vacillated from decorous to histrionic. When he auditioned for the theater's manager, the renowned and terrifying actor John Philip Kemble, he was told he was too passionate and that the character he played must always have good manners. Kemble soon made it clear that he had no confidence in him, and for a time, all the parts he was given were mute. When Cooper was finally handed the role of Malcolm in *Macbeth*, the end result was disastrous. He forgot the last two lines of the play, and backstage noise prevented him from hearing the prompter, the man hidden at the foot of stage who fed actors lines when they stumbled. The audience began to hiss, and there was such a commotion that the curtain was closed. Kemble immediately fired him, and it seemed Cooper's theater career would last only two weeks.

Undeterred, he became a strolling player, taking small parts in traveling companies until he made a successful debut in London. This led to offers playing major roles in provincial theaters. While he was playing in the fashionable resorts of Bath and Bristol, he received a letter from Wignell offering him forty weeks of employment for three years. Wignell had just persuaded Merry to join his company, and with the exit of Fennell, he needed a young leading man to match her. The money was not extraordinary, but the promise of such consistent work was alluring. Cooper's father tried to dissuade him, but the young man was determined. In 1796, he arrived in

Thomas Abthorpe Cooper. *From the University of Illinois Theatrical Print Collection.*

America at the age of twenty-four, and his first American performance was in Baltimore.

For a time, Cooper was compared to Fennell both favorably and unfavorably, but eventually, he gained his own following and star status. An early theatrical biographer described Cooper as having "a handsome face, full of the most varied expression, a noble person, a fine mellow voice of wonderful capacity for modulation, unusual dignity of manner and grace of action, and a most forcible and eloquent style of declamation." He was also greatly admired by fellow actors, like John Howard Payne, who wrote that "his whole manner is chaste, vigorous and characteristic, and his enunciation always fine." He went on to perform for three decades, and since he spent most of his career playing throughout the United States, he can be considered the bridge between the British actors who held the stage and the American-born actors to follow. Apparently, Cooper's interpretation of Hamlet was especially memorable. Multiple portraits of him in that costume prove that he was greatly associated with Shakespeare's prince. His version even marked a change in how the character was presented. Instead of keeping with the prevailing style of using modern dress for Shakespeare, Cooper wore baglike breeches and a white ruff collar like a Van Dyck portrait. Soon, this romantic style was copied by other actors.

Of all the British stars to come to America in this era, perhaps the most prominent and infamous was George Frederick Cooke. When he came to New York in 1810, he was fifty-five years old and had already had a successful career, particularly in the portrayal of villains and rakes. His first tour ended a year later in Baltimore, where he played the Holliday Street Theatre for two months and was greatly admired. At the same time, there were numerous stories about Cooke's increasingly provocative and erratic behavior. When he was not railing against "stupid actors and stupid managers," he made no secret that he was contemptuous of Americans. While in Baltimore, he visited a gentleman who shared that his family were among the first settlers in Maryland. Cooke responded by asking if he had "preserved the family jewels." When his host seemed confused by the question, Cooke clarified by saying, "The chains and handcuffs." Sometime after, when someone told Cooke that President Madison expressed an interest in going to Washington to see him perform, Cooke angrily rejected the idea, proudly boasting that he had performed for King George III. "I will not," he said, "go on for the amusement of a king of rebels, the contemptible king of the Yankee Doodles." Cooke also claimed that he fought in the British army during the Revolutionary War. The truth was that he served in the West Indies in 1795, but a couple of theater managers paid to have him discharged. It is hard to determine whether Cooke was a fantasist or a provocateur.

His bias against Americans did not translate to his romantic life. His third marriage was to an American woman, the daughter of the owner of a New York coffeehouse where actors congregated. However, a gossipy item in the *Maryland Gazette* suggested that his nuptials were an act of bigamy. In England, his first marriage to an opera singer was annulled, but his second wife returned to her family after a time, and there was no mention of a divorce. It is likely the cause of the separation was Cooke's legendary binge drinking. Unlike Cooper, who did not touch alcohol, Cooke indulged, and his career was rife with incidents in which he missed rehearsals or was visibly drunk on stage. Referring to his later years, one of Cooke's biographers wrote that "the disposition to honour his talents was opposed by his unhappy habits" and that over time, "he was no longer an agreeable associate for gentlemen, unless the bottle was kept out of sight."

Some actors defended him. James Fennell wrote in his book that "his private virtues, his charity, his general benevolence shall be opposed to one, one *only* vice he had." He went on to suggest that Cooke drank only when alcohol was offered by those who wanted him to misbehave. Still,

George Frederick Cooke, 1813. *From the Folger Shakespeare Library Digital Image Collection.*

the following oft-repeated story would seem to dispute this assertion. While acting in Dublin, a young actor named Charles Mathews was at the same lodging house as Cooke and, lingering in his doorway, was invited in for supper. As Cooke drained glass after glass of whiskey punch, he lectured the young man: "Take my word for it, there is nothing can place a man at the head of his profession but industry and sobriety." Mathews said that "his protests against drunkenness became stronger with each glass" until, fully intoxicated, he began to quiz him by performing "the passions." In this early style of acting, it was thought that if you mastered the facial expression and bodily pose of a set number of emotions (fear, anger, love, et cetera), you were equipped to play any part. Mathews angered Cooke by incorrectly guessing every passion that Cooke recreated, and when the landlady refused to give him more punch, Cooke smashed chairs and threw mirrors out of the window. When the youngster tried to leave, Cooke dragged him to the window and announced to the world that he was a murderer. The victim, he said to passersby, was the part Mathews was currently playing at the theater. As Mathews made his escape, Cooke threw a candlestick after him. Sadly, Cooke's two-year tour of America ended in New York, where he succumbed to cirrhosis of the liver. Perhaps it was best that he did not live to see England lose another war to the Americans.

Strangely, some insisted that Cooke had returned to the stage after he died. This bizarre story begins with his burial. Initially, Cooke was interred in the Stranger's Vault under St. Paul's, common practice for a person unaffiliated with a specific church. In 1821, English actor Edmund Kean, a fanatical admirer of Cooke, had his body moved outside to the center of the churchyard, along with an engraved monument to honor him. While the body was in transit, a bone fell off, which Kean took back to England and mounted on his mantel. Kean believed it to be the finger that Cooke used to gesture, an inspiring symbol of the man's skill. Kean's wife, however, did not feel the same kinship to the dead actor and had her maid toss the finger into a river.

Before Cooke's body was finally put to rest, Dr. John Francis, Cooke's physician, claimed to have removed the actor's head because he was anxious to study the physiology of genius. Later, Francis said he lent Cooke's skull to a production of *Hamlet* at the Park Theatre, where he had a box on opening nights. If true, there was a beautiful symmetry to its use. Cooke once bragged that since his earliest days as a boy actor, he had played every part in *Hamlet*, even Ophelia and the queen. "One day, I'll play Yorick, too," he proclaimed, "and make the thing complete."

After Dr. Francis died, Cooke's skull changed hands and finally came into the possession of the Jefferson Medical College Library in Philadelphia. The story should have ended there, but some continued to hold the unlikely belief that the skull stayed in the properties room of the Park and was used by other Hamlets until the theater burned down in 1848. The legend of the missing skull must have continued to live on. In 1873, a strange man appeared in the office of a New York theater manager and tried to sell him Cooke's skull wrapped in paper. Even today, stories of Cooke's headless ghost roaming the churchyard are still repeated during haunted ghost tours and in books about macabre New York locations.

Another popular English actor was Charles Mathews, the object of Cooke's drunken rant, who eventually carved out a fine career for himself as a comic actor. He was known mostly for his work as a monologist in what he called his "At Home" series. Mathews would enter a bare stage with only a table and chair. Then, pretending to be a traveler, he would portray a variety of comic characters he "met" along the way and would perform a number of songs. With a variety of simple quick changes, he would play both men and women and was admired for the realism of his creations. Comparing the differences between pirated printings of his material, it is clear that Mathews was always making changes and allowed for improvisation when in front of an audience.

Mathews landed in America in 1822. Wishing to avoid an outbreak of yellow fever in New York, he decided to move south and perform until the danger passed. In his travels, he struggled with American manners, which were not as sharply defined by class differences as they were in England. In a letter to his wife, he accused Americans of "studied sullenness, the determination never to be civil or apparently kind to a fellow-creature, and not to bow, or say thank ye, to a person they know to be their superior, for they affect not to believe in it." When he arrived in Baltimore for his American debut, he presented *A Trip to Paris*, one of what he called his "monopolylogues," at the Holliday Street Theatre, where construction was almost complete. While he expected his audiences to be dull, to his delight, he found them to be intelligent and enormously appreciative— even better than audiences in London—and he was forced to revise his opinion of Americans. They are "heavy and grave," he wrote, "but not so in the theatre."

Mathews went on to create another collection titled *A Trip to America*, inspired by people he met during his tour of the eastern seaboard. There was the enslaved Agamemnon; a Kentucky shoemaker named Colonel Hiram Peglar; a French emigrant tailor called Monsieur Capot; Miss Mangelwurzel, the Dutch heiress; and Mr. O'Sullivan, an Irish "improver." This time, not all of his characters landed with the public. Especially reviled by some was his Yankee, a gun-toting slave dealer from Vermont named Jonathan Doubikins, who talked about liberty and equality while periodically hitting an enslaved person whenever he got mad. This social satire was lost on some. Articles and essays were written, taking apart every detail of his portrayal from the fact that there was no slave trade in New England to Mathews's inappropriate wearing of a straw hat, an unauthentic choice for a Yankee.

One of his comic targets was very specific. Mathews portrayed a character named Caesar Alcibiades Hannibal Hewlett, the "Kentucky Roscius," a Black actor who would butcher lines from Shakespeare (example: "Now is de vinter of our discontent made glorus summer by de son of New-York"). This was obviously a sendup of Black actor James Hewlett, who performed at the African Grove in New York, an important early theater for Black audiences. This cartoonish depiction was especially hurtful to Hewlett, because when the two had met, Mathews had requested that Hewlitt perform several speeches and was apparently complimentary. In response, Hewlitt composed an open letter to the actor to point out his betrayal:

An array of Charles Mathews's characters. *Courtesy of the Garrick Club, London.*

You have, I perceive by the programme of your performance, ridiculed our African Theatre on Mercer-street and burlesqued me with the rest of the negro actors, as you are pleased to call us—mimicked our styles—imitated our dialects—laughed at our anomalies—and lampooned, O shame, even our complexions. Was this well for a brother actor?

Mathews never responded to Hewlett and ended up spinning some of his American characters from *A Trip to America* into another popular play, *Jonathan in England*. The premise was that Doubikins, along with the enslaved Agamemnon, travel to England to improve his knowledge of English affairs. Since few in England could afford to make the journey to America, Mathews's exaggerated take on American behaviors would be accepted as genuine and live in the English imagination for some time. In fact, the play was praised as a means of bringing greater understanding between the two countries.

MOBOCRACY

Antebellum theater could be a raucous affair. Audience behavior was not passive and could range from polite to inconsiderate to openly hostile. The most common complaints were men not taking off their hats during shows and noxious cigarette and cigar smoke. One French tourist visiting Baltimore criticized the ladies in boxes who sat on the edge and turned their backs to the stage to converse. His indignation was not surprising. In Paris, the custom in the pit was to shame anyone who exhibited these behaviors—even allowing a shawl to hang from your box would be greeted by continuous shouts until the offending item was stowed or the police were called to correct the offensive behavior.

For American audiences, the biggest disruptions were caused by young unmarried men. Whistling, stamping, spitting and fighting were not uncommon among male audience members. Soon after opening, the Theatre and Circus complained of several riots in the third tier of the gallery, some caused by neighborhood gangs, such as the New Towners, Pointers and Hillen Streeters.[21] It was said their favorite game was to "bring abandoned drunken females to the Theatre, and place them in the second tier of boxes, among the ladies, and then display as much insolent bravado as was possible." While it is true that many disturbances came from the galleries populated by the working class, firsthand accounts have revealed that many originated from the wealthier boxes as well.

Baltimore's first recorded riot was in 1807 when a doctor, tired of teaching young surgeons in his home, built an operating studio for the dissection of cadavers. When news got out that bodies were being taken from graves, a mob, appalled by the desecration, burned the structure to the ground. In 1812, after James Madison signed a declaration of war against the United Kingdom, an antiwar pro-British federalist newspaper was attacked by Republican supporters, and the paper's office and printing press were destroyed. Mob action against the publishers continued for weeks until they had to be held in Baltimore Prison for their protection. But safety was not to be found. A group of roughly three hundred surrounded the prison, and the cells were somehow opened. When the publishers tried to push through the crowd to escape, they were viciously attacked. They were beaten with fists and clubs, penknives were jabbed in their faces, hot candle grease was poured into their eyes and their clothing was torn and cut off. From this point on, the nickname "mobtown" stuck, and despite offended Baltimoreans pointing out riots in other cities, the city could not shake the name.

Two of the city's theaters would become part of this legacy of violence. When Edmund Kean arrived in New York in 1825, there was great anticipation from American audiences. He was considered the greatest tragedian since David Garrick and displayed a great deal of charm and eloquence. People clamored to see him, and tickets were scalped for exorbitant sums. Still, most newspapers seemed to want to put him in his place by writing savage reviews. In the past, they had celebrated the abrasive George Frederick Cooke, but after the War of 1812, the ground had shifted toward cultural independence, and Kean's Englishness and high pay made him a very visible target. Still, he found admirers despite those prejudices. A stage manager at a New York theater wrote to a friend in Dublin about his grudging admiration for the actor:

> *Kean is with us & playing to great business: he averages about $1000 a Night—the people don't know exactly what to make of him—his strange manner surprises them but his style gains converts every night & before he leaves us, I expect they will be unanimous in calling him as they express it the greatest creature they ever saw. We find him extremely agreeable in the Theatre & are agreeably disappointed in finding him in manner and conduct exactly the reverse of what we expected.*

In 1821, Kean played Baltimore for fourteen nights as part of his tour, and according to manager William Wood, his popularity led to a new custom to be adopted in the United States—the curtain call:

The advent of Kean…led subsequently to much annoyance and to many abuses. I allude to the habit of calling out performers, dead or alive, and after the curtain has dropped, to receive a tribute to extra applause. The absurdity of dragging out before the curtain a deceased Hamlet, Macbeth, or Richard in an exhausted state, merely to make a bow…is one which we date with us from this time.

Even actors would complain about this new practice. Nevertheless, it became a staple of the theatrical experience.

After Baltimore, Kean headed for Boston for a second time. Managers tried to deter him from performing because it was the off season and many people were out of town, but Kean insisted. After a few badly attended shows, he arrived at the theater to find only a few seats filled. He could not be convinced to perform for such a small house and went to his hotel. However, at the last minute, the boxes suddenly started filling up. Word was sent to Kean, but he would not budge and left town the next morning.

Boston newspapers considered his absence an enormous slight. One called his behavior a "specimen of rude superciliousness," and another wrote that "all persons are cautioned against harboring the aforesaid vagrant.…As he has violated his pledged faith to me, I deem it my duty thus to put my neighbors on their guard against him." The New York papers piled on, and Kean did not help himself with the feeble explanation he sent to the *National Advocate*: "I counted twenty persons in front of the theater. I then decided, hastily if you please, that it was better to husband my resources for a more favourable season." As hostility mounted, Kean abandoned plans for an extended tour and headed back to England.

Later, the discovery of a scandalous affair with an alderman's wife caused Kean to lose the British public's favor. Needing money and feeling his health deteriorating, he decided on another American tour in 1825, presumably to recapture his early success. It would not be an easy task. Even before he arrived, the New York press had cast him as a reprobate and saw an opportunity for a moral crusade. Some encouraged a boycott, which sparked a debate over what we would call "cancel culture" today. Some questioned whether we need moral virtue from our entertainers. Others rejected Kean's many apologies and believed that taking away his livelihood should be a consequence of his actions. A huge audience showed up for his appearance at the Park Theatre, and many attended just to interrupt the performance. When Kean came out on stage, shouting from the boxes ensured no one would hear him speak.

Edmund Kean as Richard III. *From the University of Illinois Theatrical Print Collection.*

Although the rest of Kean's New York appearances were uneventful, when he traveled to Boston, he would receive a far worse reception than the one he received his first night in New York. Before the show began, he tried to deliver another apology, but pandemonium followed. A chorus of voices ensured he would not be heard, and he was pelted with nuts and other projectiles, driving him from the stage and the theater. Unfortunately, halting the play led to a full-blown riot. Threats to Kean's life were shouted, while windows, chandeliers and seats were destroyed.

His next engagements in Philadelphia and New York were without incident, so he must have felt the worst was over. He committed to playing Richard III for eight nights at the Holliday Street Theatre, a decision he would soon regret. Initially, Kean's first night in Baltimore had every indication that it was going to be positive. His supporters hung signs from the boxes that read, "Let the Friends of Kean be silent," and, "Kean for ever!" but it soon became clear that another faction, eager to punish the actor, had come to disrupt the evening. When Kean took the stage as the villainous prince, he was given three rounds of applause, but before he could speak, chaos broke out. Others began to hiss and scream, and Kean was struck in the leg by a twist of tobacco. The actor tried to address the mostly male audience but to no avail. William Wood recollected:

> The greatest portion of the female auditors retired in disgust from the disgraceful scene, and the play at length ended in noise and confusion. Warren conducted the ladies of the company through the crowd without molestation; Kean was conveyed through the adjoining house to his lodgings safely, but in extreme terror, as might well be expected; for in some expressions uttered by the rioters, it was fairly inferred that personal violence would be offered by them.

To make matters worse, before the show began, Kean's fans, eager to support their hero, grabbed anyone they deemed a threat to his performance and dragged them out of the theater. Those ejected men stayed outside and began gathering others with their tale of mistreatment; it was clear they intended to storm the theater and attack the actor. After a brickbat was thrown through the window of the theater's saloon, Mayor John Montgomery and his bailiffs stood at the entrance and waylaid them. Considering that every carriage was being searched in pursuit of the actor, Montgomery probably saved Kean's life by giving him time to escape.

The consequence of the riot was the closing of the theater and the cancellation of the season. This decision angered some, who threatened the theater with harm, so a watch had to be placed outside. Kean took a steamboat back to Philadelphia and never returned to Baltimore. The next Kean to appear in the city was his son, Charles, who arrived five years later. Still, there was one positive outcome of Edmund Kean's time on Holliday Street. Incidents such as this one seemed to finally change the public's perception of him from a hopelessly immoral man to an ill-treated one, and the antagonism toward him faded.

This would not be the last time an audience's animosity would be directed toward an English actor in Baltimore. The bombardment and attempted invasion of the city during the War of 1812 left deep wounds. German and Irish immigrants brought their own antipathies, and England's stance against slavery did not endear itself to the city's pro-Southern, proslavery factions. This bad feeling was reignited when a British actor named Joshua Anderson allegedly made unkind remarks about Americans. Accounts were sketchy. One said he referred to "blasted Yankees" at a table in a hotel. Another claimed it happened on a steamboat. Yet another said that he hurled insults about his host country from the stage. From 1831 to 1832, several of his performances in New York had to be canceled due to patriotic mobs who objected to his presence. Mainly, this was the work of the Bowery Boys, a gang that ruled the theater from the gallery by throwing apples, nuts and gingerbread at the middle- and upper-class audiences in the pit.

In 1833, Anderson was booked at the Adelphi. Anticipating trouble, the following mea culpa was published days before he opened:

> *Mr. Anderson, from a series of unfortunate circumstances, having been deprived of the opportunity of exercising his profession, is induced to make one appeal to the Citizens of Baltimore, trusting that for, any offense he may have committed, the punishment he has already received may be considered sufficient. In the full hope of this indulgence he throws himself upon the liberality of the American Public.*

On the night of the performance, trouble was brewing outside as people made their way to their seats. A crowd had gathered outside, and one eyewitness wrote that it was "composed of elements that only needed a wink or snap of the finger and thumb to send them to their work of mischief." After the first few notes of the overture were played, a rock was thrown through a window and struck an instrument. Soon, projectiles started coming through all the windows; the doorkeeper was soon pushed aside, and the mob stormed the theater. A rattled Thomas Walton, one of the managers, tried to calm the crowd and pleaded with them not to destroy his property, but the rioters laughed and swarmed the stage. Scenery was cut with knives, and some rioters banged on the drum that was used to simulate the sound of thunder backstage. Others looted items from the actors' trunks. As Walton saw someone about to set the scenery on fire, he pleaded:

> *Fellow-citizens, I assure you, on my honor, that the fellow Anderson is not in the house. The ladies of the company have all gone to their homes, the orchestra has ignobly fled, and I am left alone. Take your seats and I will sing you "A Wet Sheet and a Flowing Sea," and dance "Fisher's Hornpipe," if anyone will be so kind as to whistle for me.*

Hope was restored when one of the throng enthusiastically jumped on stage to accompany him. After the completion of Walton's impromptu performance, the rioters, now in a better humor, gave him three cheers and left. The next day, the theater managers released a statement, asking for stolen items to be returned and saying that any damage done to the theater would not prevent the next scheduled performance. As the saying goes, the show must go on.

Rehearsal for a Riot

These events, although chaotic and potentially grave, would not come close to what happened at a New York theater in 1849. More than 20 people died, and 150 were wounded or injured in front of the Astor Place Opera House, the greatest loss of civilian life since the Revolution. What is especially surprising about the bloodshed was that it was triggered by a rivalry between two famous dramatic actors. One was Edwin Forrest, an American who was enormously popular with middle and lower-class audiences. The other was William Macready, a visiting Englishman praised by New York's cultural elite. In the telling of this tragic event, what usually goes unmentioned is that Baltimore helped set the stage for the deadly clash, one that exemplified class tensions during the post-Jacksonian era.

Edwin Forrest was born in Philadelphia in 1806 to a poor family, a fact that he would repeat throughout his life to emphasize his status as a self-made man. He seemed to have no formal schooling, but his father, a runner for a bank, was eager for Edwin's advancement and used his modest income to pay for some tutoring and elocution lessons. Edwin's brother, William, first exposed him to the stage when he took him to see Thomas Cooper's portrayal of Hamlet at the Chestnut Street Theatre. Inspired, the two formed a thespian club that met in the back of a tavern. The pair even performed a show as amateurs in a local theater.

Edwin's father died of tuberculosis when he was thirteen, so to help the family stay afloat, he held various jobs in a warehouse, an import house, an anti-Federalist newspaper and a cooper shop. Still determined to become an actor and tired of being seen as physically weak, Edwin developed a regiment to train his body by walking on his hands, performing acrobatics and doing exercises to expand his voice. His obsession with physical fitness would continue throughout his life, and he would often refer to himself as Hercules. Forrest could never be accused of excessive humility.

His first break happened because he attended a demonstration of nitrous oxide. When the crowd was asked for a volunteer, and young Forrest stepped forward to inhale the gas and then recited speeches from plays for fifteen minutes. A colonel and future Philadelphia mayor named John Swift was so impressed by the boy's talent that he asked William Wood to feature him in a juvenile role at his Walnut Street Theatre. Forrest performed for three nights, and despite a very favorable notice from one of the local papers, he was not offered continued employment. He was forced to go back to other jobs to support his family.

Eventually, he was contracted to work for a small theater company that serviced Pittsburgh, Lexington and Cincinnati. It was a ramshackle existence that lasted only a year, and Forrest was always broke. After working for other failing theater companies, including a stint with Pépin and Breschard's touring circus, he finally landed steady acting work in New Orleans. It was there that he became an audience favorite while having a series of colorful friendships with a duelist, a Choctaw Native and the soon to be famous Jim Bowie. Eventually, he found himself in Albany, where he played supporting roles for a touring Edmund Kean, who gave the young man his stamp of approval. When Forrest made his way to New York in 1825, he was unemployed and penniless, but his luck changed when a fellow actor saw him sitting outside a theater. Remembering his fine reputation in Albany, he recommended Forrest for a benefit at the Park Theatre. After playing dates in Philadelphia, Washington and Baltimore, he signed a contract with the Bowery Theatre and achieved immediate popularity. Reviewers admired his athleticism and deep voice and compared him favorably to Thomas Cooper, as well as another prominent English actor named William Macready.

Macready was aware of Forrest. When he was doing his first tour of America in 1826, he saw Forrest play the role of William Tell. Macready thought he showed great promise but saw much room for growth. He wrote in his diary that Forrest "was gifted with extraordinary strength of limb, to which he omitted no opportunity of giving prominence" but "had not rightly understood passages in his text" and needed "a severe study of his art."

Macready began his career playing villains, but in time, he came to be known for roles in Shakespearean plays, such as *Hamlet*, *King Lear* and *Richard II*. In contrast to Forrest's hypermasculine and instinctive performances beloved by the "Bowery lads," Macready, although capable of great emotion, was more intellectual and controlled.

In his travels, Macready's experiences with Americans were mixed. He wrote that he found American audiences to be "less sensitive and more phlegmatic" than English ones, but overall, he found Americans to be quite civil. Nevertheless, he soon found out how easy it was to test American pride when he appeared in *William Tell* at the Holliday Street Theatre in 1827. In the fourth act, a corrupt governor forces Tell to shoot an apple on top of his son's head. If he refuses, both Tell and his son will be executed. Before he takes the crucial shot, Tell rejects one of the arrows because it is bent and snaps it in a dramatic moment. However, a fake arrow was not provided, so Macready was forced to use one of the special arrows from his quiver. When Macready confronted the property man backstage, Macready said, "I can't get such an arrow in your country, sir!" This was interpreted as an insult to America, and anonymous letters were sent to the press to make sure Macready was chastised. When Macready read the complaints, he assembled the cast and apologized if he had personally offended anyone. Luckily for him, the incident did not lead to audience protests.

By the time Macready toured again in 1843, Forrest had become a nationwide star in a time when English actors continued to overshadow homegrown talent. His popularity was such that in 1838, the Democratic Party sought to capitalize on it by having him deliver the main speech at the national convention instead of Martin Van Buren, the president and party leader. In addition to his fame, Forrest had also become a figurehead for championing American playwrighting. He used his newfound wealth to hold several contests, and the result was two very popular and heroic leading roles he played for most of his career. The first was in *Metamora or the Last of the Wampanoags* (1829), by John Augustus Stone, which took place in seventeenth-century New England. It depicted a Native chief who fought against the oppression of the English settlers. Another winner was *The Gladiator* (1831), by Robert Bird, which gave Forrest the opportunity to play Spartacus, an enslaved man battling the forces of Rome. In spite of its setting, it was celebrated for being an American production of an American play with American actors.[22] In Baltimore, Forrest played both parts to crowded houses at both the Holliday and Front Street Theatres.

Macready's extensive tour was successful overall. Audiences were appreciative, and he was embraced by polite society, including Forrest, who left a good impression. Macready wrote, "I like all I see of Forrest very much. He appears a clear-headed, honest, kind man; what can be better?" Around this time, Macready was asked by a Philadelphia theater manager to play the same part as Forrest on alternate nights. Macready wisely declined.

In 1846, what might have been described as a friendly rivalry turned into a public feud. When Forrest traveled to Europe to perform, he saw Macready play Hamlet at the Edinburgh Theatre. Attempting to put his own spin on the character, the Englishman added what Forrest called "a fancy dance" to one scene, and Forrest hissed to show his displeasure. In Shakespeare's play, Hamlet sees the king and queen coming to watch a group of actors perform and says, "They are coming to the play; I must be idle." Another interpretation of the word *idle* is strange, so Macready paraded around the stage in a bizarre fashion to support the idea that Hamlet was feigning insanity. Forrest either revealed his lack of formal education by misunderstanding Macready's intentions or, having his own heroic conception of the character, found the choice unmanly.

The hot-tempered Macready was incensed, but Forrest was unapologetic. He insisted that it was retribution for Macready prompting his friends to hiss at him during one of his poorly received Covent Garden performances. Macready denied organizing any such action, and the result was that both sides of the Atlantic took sides about who was the wronged party. In retrospect, the tensions between them seemed inevitable. For twenty years prior, newspapers had pitted them against each other by making comparisons. Predictably, American papers found Macready to be talented but said that Forrest was his superior. In 1838, the *Baltimore Sun* pronounced that Macready "does not read better, his gestures are not more graceful and appropriate, and nature has not given him the physical energy with which she has more completely endowed Forrest." The *Sun* sang Forrest's praises again in 1843: "The acting of the one was a display of the tact of an artist, with talent and genius of a high order, the other all the tact, but not the feeling, all the act, but not the genius, all the tameness, but not the power."

Left: Edwin Forrest as Macbeth. *From the Folger Shakespeare Library Digital Image Collection.*

Right: Charles Macready as Macbeth. *From the Folger Shakespeare Library Digital Image Collection.*

When Macready returned to tour America in 1848, he was seemingly on top of the world. To honor his departure, the queen had requested a command performance, and he was seriously contemplating a permanent move to the United States. This optimism would soon fade after he gave his first performance in New York. After his bow, Macready made the mistake of alluding to his quarrel with Forrest while thanking the audience for their warm reception. This did not sit well with Forrest supporters, who were determined to punish Macready on his behalf.

Forrest then embarked on the pettiest of plans. Clearly looking to goad Macready, he used his star power to secure engagements in the same cities where Macready was appearing and insisted on playing the same roles. When Macready finally arrived in Baltimore so did his spiteful shadow. One city historian reflected that "there was hardly a small boy in the city that did not have an opinion," and seeing both actors perform "was hardly thought of by the majority, who would have considered it treason to either favorite to be seen among the adherents of his rival." Ironically, Macready performed Hamlet at the Front Street Theatre despite the venue's history with the kind of working-class audiences that followed Forrest. It was there that the Englishman, repulsed by the institution of slavery, was given a real skull to use as a prop, one that had belonged to an enslaved man who had been hanged for killing his overseer. At the Holliday Street Theatre, Forrest also played Hamlet, and both would play the titular role in *Richelieu* (1839), a play about the scheming and powerful cardinal of France.

The appearances of both actors were well attended and enthusiastic. Forrest's audiences were described as "intelligent and fashionable," and the review of Macready's performance made a point of reporting the large number of women in the audience. This usually was given as a sign of an audience's overall respectability, since men would typically see a show and, once its suitability was determined, return with their wives. Macready's friends in the city insisted that since he received just as much praise from audiences as Forrest, he had won a great victory. Struck by the absurdity of these events, Macready wrote in his diary, "Victory? over what or whom?"

Baltimore would be the last stop of this head-to-head competition. Macready escaped Forrest's reach by doing a southern tour, but a stop in Cincinnati assured him that the squabble was not over; an audience member threw half a sheep's carcass on stage, much to the horror of the beleaguered actor. Of course, the real trouble came when Macready returned to New York. On May 10, 1849, he was to play Macbeth at the Astor Place Opera House, located in a wealthy neighborhood where expensive carriages and white gloves were the norm. Forrest chose to play the same character blocks away at the Bowery Theatre, a place that claimed Forrest as their champion. Now well-organized, Forrest supporters filled the Astor Place Opera House, heckled Macready and threw food and chairs until he withdrew from the stage.

Abandoning his goal of becoming an American, Macready announced his return to England, but members of the city's elite convinced him to return the next evening. This decision outraged the Bowery Boys. Posters were printed, asking working men whether "Americans or English Rule in this City?" And it was obvious the rioters were coming back in force. The police and militia were called in, and violence broke out both inside and outside the theater. According to one chronicler, paving stones were thrown, shots were fired and soon, "the wounded, the dying, and the dead, were scattered in every direction." When the ghastly scene was over, Macready boarded a ship, never to return.

The consequences of the violence at Astor Place were long lasting when it came to bringing Shakespeare to the public. Before the riot, his work belonged to all audiences, rich and poor, because it was a staple of the English repertoire. After the riot, respectable actors began to avoid playing in working-class theaters, which led to the perception that Shakespeare was for elites only, a false conclusion that still exists today.

In retrospect, it is surprising that there was no serious trouble in Baltimore over Forrest and Macready, especially considering the city's past bouts of violent patriotic fervor. The reason could be that sentiments in the city were beginning to shift. Nativist societies had begun to form, and in 1844, the *Baltimore Clipper* threw its support behind the local American Republican Party that wanted the "banishment of foreign influences and spreading of American feeling and interests." It is possible that the anger and resentment focused on the British was slowly being transferred to Irish Catholic immigrants who were showing up in the city in greater numbers. These attitudes grew even larger in the 1850s, when secret societies such as the "Sons of the Sires" and the "Order of the Star Spangled Banner" were formed. When members were questioned about their activities, the response was an evasive "I know nothing." This led to the formation of the Know Nothing Party, which would yield considerable power in the city. In 1854, Know Nothing candidate Samuel Hinks beat a Democrat to become the mayor of Baltimore. That same year, Monsignor Bedini, an envoy of the pope, who was visiting the city, was burned in effigy by a group of men in Monument Square.

"Petticoat Government"

In 1848, comic actor turned theater manager Charles D.S. Howard advertised for "ladies and gentlemen of the histrionic profession" to apply to what he called the Howard Athenaeum and Gallery of Fine Arts. This comprised the top two floors of a building on the northeast corner of Baltimore and Charles Streets. The stage was fifty feet wide and twenty-six feet deep; it had two tiers of boxes and sat between eight hundred and one thousand people. As usual, a saloon was provided. Seats still cost only twenty-five cents, and private boxes cost two dollars. Order, respectability and racial discrimination were primary concerns. A notice stated that gentlemen who came without ladies were charged extra, unaccompanied ladies could not attend and Black patrons were prohibited.

Howard assembled a solid but unremarkable company and began presenting serious plays, comedies, farces and burlettas (a kind of short comic opera). After only a year, Edmund Peale took over and tried to bring his museum aesthetic to the space by exhibiting panoramic views of the United States. Assembled with large panels that surrounded and immersed the viewer, these installations can be considered an early form of virtual reality.

After Peale withdrew in 1853, New York actor George Joseph Arnold tried to make a go of it. Although he had a history of playing in tragedies and melodramas, he presented comedies and farces in what he now called Arnold's Olympic Theatre. Arnold spent $12,000 expanding the saloon but, like Howard and Peale, could not make the theater profitable, so he left Baltimore to avoid his creditors. At this point, the Olympic was not considered a first-rate house, but this would soon change when Laura Keene, a talented and energetic English actress, began her illustrious career as a theater manager.

Born Mary Frances Moss in Westminster, she was the youngest of four children born to a successful builder and a mother who made sure she took lessons in dance, piano and voice. Always precocious, Mary Frances was a voracious reader and spent long hours with her uncle, a painter who recognized her talent when she picked up a brush. After her father died, Mary Frances took a job as a waitress in a local pub to support the family. Soon, her beauty and vivaciousness captured the attention of a dashing army officer named Henry Taylor, the godson of the Duke of Wellington. Mary Frances's brother had just been lost at sea, and Taylor offered security and protection at a time when there were few choices for poor women. After their wedding, Taylor bought a tavern, and Mary Frances became a barmaid. After seven years, she was the mother of two young daughters and was still doing the same job. It must have been obvious to her that a more comfortable life was not going to materialize.

A catastrophic event would soon change her life forever. Mary Frances's husband committed a felony so egregious that he was sent to a penal colony in Australia. Instead of going back to the tavern, the twenty-five-year-old decided to make a radical transformation. Her aunt Elizabeth, an actress with some connections, trained her for the stage, and she adopted a new name to go with her new identity, Laura Keene. She must have been a mix of great talent and discipline, because after a very short time, she opened in Richmond as Juliet in *Romeo and Juliet*. She was so successful in the part that she quickly acquired a London engagement—quite a feat for a beginner. Madame Vestris, who managed the Lyceum Theatre with her husband, Charles Mathews, soon lured Keene to join her acting company as a featured player and made a point of promoting her by putting her photograph in print shops. During her time with Vestris, Keene must have

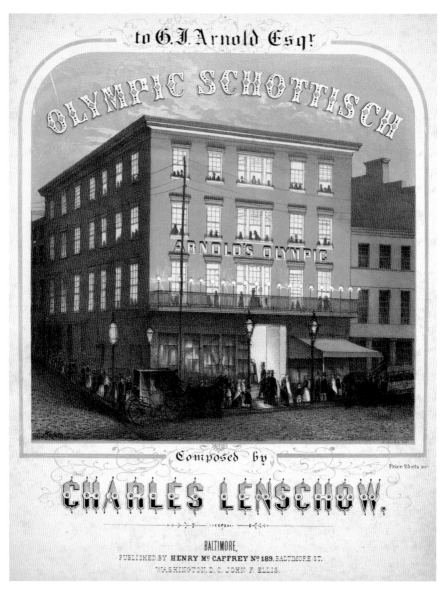

Arnold's Olympic Theatre, 1853. *Courtesy the Lester S. Levy Collection of Sheet Music, Sheridan Libraries, Johns Hopkins University.*

observed how she created lavish productions with realistic costumes and settings. She had been an innovator since the 1830s, when she introduced "the box set" to England, a series of walls to suggest an interior instead of a single painted curtain.

Keene was soon noticed by a New York manager named James William Wallack who was so impressed that he offered her a position at his theater. Since Vestris and Mathews were having money troubles, she found Wallack's proposal too good to pass up, so she tearfully left her children and boarded a ship for America. New York audiences immediately embraced her as a star, praising her looks, aristocratic manner and clear voice. By all accounts, she had a natural style that set her apart from earlier actors and was an extremely good comedian. Keene went on to perform thirty-four leading roles in a year and a half—an astonishing output. Now that her future seemed secure, she called for her mother and children.

At forty-five dollars a week, Keene was paid a paltry sum for the value she brought to the theater. She wanted more money to support her family but could not reveal why. Her looks and the promise of her romantic availability was too valuable in an age when the majority of audiences were men and their support was needed for benefits; the existence of her still-legal marriage and two daughters would have to remain a secret. Just before the beginning of her second season, Keene saw a notice in the newspaper that the Olympic Theatre in Baltimore was available for lease. Bristling to be free of Wallack and a cantankerous leading man, she decided to become a manager and control her own destiny. This was a daring move considering that men at the time spoke wryly of "petticoat government," which suggested that women were incapable of sound leadership.

When she arrived in Baltimore in 1853, Keene immediately remodeled the theater to make it more comfortable and assembled a top-notch company composed of actors from New York, Boston and Philadelphia. She promised content "of the most refined character" as well as promising "all the requisite Scenery, Costumes of the period, Appointments, appropriate Mountings, and the most minute attention to the general 'Mise en Scene.'" A fellow manager later said of Keene that she "could take a piece of paste-board, a pencil and calipers, and in an hour's time furnish drawings of stage settings or scenes for new plays for her stage manager, scene painter and head carpenter, such as could not be conceived or thought of by any other actor or actress in the business."

The rechristened Charles Street Theatre opened on December 24 with a drama followed by short comedies. Despite her theater's proximity to the more established Baltimore Museum, Keene was immediately celebrated by Baltimore newspapers, which determined that her theater was "destined to become one of our most fashionable resorts." She became such a household name in Baltimore that she had a brand of chewing tobacco named after her.

Laura Keene, circa 1855. *From the National Portrait Gallery, Smithsonian Institution; acquired through the generosity of Bill and Sally Wittliff.*

By the end of the season, Keene, usually a well of energy, was exhausted. Moreover, she got word from an investigator that her husband had turned up in California, and she was anxious to seek a divorce. This probably prompted her to take an opportunity in San Francisco. With a final performance in *As*

You Like It in March, she left the city and would not return until 1856, when she played the Holliday Street Theatre with a touring company she created.

Keene's innovations as a manager are often overlooked by historians. Her business acumen, attention to detail and more realistic style of theatrical design were important, but she also standardized the Saturday matinee performance and the long-run show, the practice of running a successful production until it was no longer profitable instead of following a strict calendar. After Keene's departure, the Charles Street Theatre was rented by various actors and minstrel show companies, which led to lawsuits for unpaid renovations. By 1859, the theater was renamed "The Hall" and was used for religious services until it became a warehouse and then an office space. The building was torn down in 1880.

JOHN E. OWENS AND *UNCLE TOM'S CABIN* (S)

In 1841, showman P.T. Barnum outmaneuvered Edmund Peale to purchase the decaying Scudder's Museum in New York. Renamed Barnum's American Museum, its exhibits were expanded, and entertainments were offered, making it one of the most popular destinations of its kind. Barnum was looking to expand; his original plan for Baltimore had been to open a competing operation and drive Peale's Museum out of business, but four years later, Peale's financial woes allowed Barnum to purchase the museum outright and install his uncle to manage it.[23] The Baltimore Museum would get no dramatic transformation. When it came to running the theater—still no more than a lecture hall—no significant changes were made. There was no noticeable alteration in the choice of plays or its resident stock company, and Barnum's uncle died six months later. It would be subsequent managers who took the venue in new directions.

One of these managers was comedian John E. Owens, who was more associated with the museum than any other performer. Born in Liverpool, England, in 1823, he and his family moved to Philadelphia when he was five. He received a quality education at the best schools and was judged to be a good student, even though on "recitation days," he would act out his lessons with a cane and spectacles. His love for theater blossomed when he read *Richard III* and a gothic farce based on a Washington Irving story called *The Spectre Bridegroom*. He went to the theater only twice, but after sitting near the stage and being spellbound by the spectacle of *The Forty Thieves*, he was bitten by the show business bug. In 1840, he was a pharmacist's apprentice but was determined to abandon that life for the stage. One day, a notice in the local paper caught his eye. The National Theatre in Philadelphia was looking for "supers" (short for "supernumeraries"), and the seventeen-year-old was hired. At the time, the National was run by William Burton, a popular comedian who specialized in physical comedy. He was interested in building a solid company instead of participating in the star system adopted by other theaters. Owens did not say a word to his parents about his new career. They eventually discovered his name in the newspaper, which listed the actors in the show. Fortunately for him, instead of condemning his new profession, they encouraged him to continue.

It was common practice for a young actor in a company to be tutored by a seasoned veteran. If Burton was not his teacher, at the very least, he would have noticed Burton's meticulous approach to creating individualized comic characters. But that education took time, and Owens was not an instant success. After one performance in which he flubbed his lines by saying them in the wrong act, he tried to quit, but Burton saw him on the street and insisted the young man return. "You must walk," Burton said, "before you can run." What came next must have made Owens believe fate was at work. While working his way up to becoming a supporting comedian, he played a pharmacist's apprentice in a play called *The Ocean Child*, and during a tour, he appeared in *The Spectre Bridegroom* at the Holliday Street Theatre, no doubt the fulfillment of a boyhood dream.

In 1844, he was noticed by Edmund Peale, who hired him for one season at the Baltimore Museum for fourteen dollars a week and two benefits.[24] The public's reaction was uniformly positive, and his popularity increased. Apparently, crowds were turned away when he played a rustic Yankee character named Jemmy Twitcher as the comic relief in a melodrama called *The Golden Farmer*, a part previously played by Burton. Owens, like Burton, took his art form seriously and was not always comfortable competing with Peale's curiosities. One time, the young actor put his foot down when he found out he shared billing on a billboard with a live bear that was to be displayed on the roof. However, his complaint became moot when the unfortunate bear became sickly and died.

After another season in Philadelphia and New Orleans, Owens returned to the Museum for the 1847 season.[25] It was now under new management, which had modified the lecture hall into a true theater by lowering it by a floor and adding three tiers of boxes. By this time, Owens felt great kinship with the city, probably because of the warm welcome he always received, and decided to remain for an extended period. During his apprenticeship and his tenure

OWENS

"His life was laughter, and the ludicrous
So mix'd in him, that nature might stand up,
And say to all the world—this was an actor.

A lithograph of John E. Owens.
From the Folger Shakespeare Library
Digital Image Collection.

at the Baltimore Museum, he would share the stage with a who's who of major mid-century talents, some known to students of theater history (T.D. Rice, Charlotte Cushman, the Keans, Edwin Forrest, Charles Macready and Joseph Jefferson), as well as others who are not so commonly discussed (E.L. Davenport, J.W. Wallack, Fanny Wallack, Kate Ludlow, James Murdock and Junius Brutus Booth).

Owens eventually decided to try his hand at management by renting the Charles Street Theatre and assembled a short season. He then bought a share of the museum, and by 1850, he owned it entirely. Now the full proprietor, he encouraged local talent when he could, but the results were sometimes mixed. As the curtain fell on one of his shows, the playwright, a Baltimore lawyer, emerged from the audience and railed against the theater because the actors were "imperfect in their parts." He complained that he did not recognize his play due to alterations and omissions. Owens came forward and defended the actors by saying cuts had been made where the text was not fit for public consumption, and if they doubted it, they could go the box office and read the script. That was the last performance of the play.

After eight years of performing in Baltimore, Owens was now a star, despite the fact that he disliked being treated like one. Perhaps he needed a break from the headaches of management or wanted to see if he could succeed in New York, the country's theatrical center. In any event, Owens decided to sell the museum to businessman Henry C. Jarrett for $15,000 in 1851 and left to appear at a newly built theater on Broadway. Jarrett, a Baltimore native who had been an amateur actor, was known as "the railroad manager." He chartered a fast train so that nervous actors who were in the museum's opening play could race to Washington to appear in an afterpiece at his other theater, the National, and return the same night. He also became well known for his grandiose advertising at the museum. For a production of *Aladdin*, he had a twenty-five-foot-tall balloon with the play's name in giant letters created and fixed to the roof. Regardless of these practices, it can be argued that the most important decision made under Jarrett's management was the presentation of the first theatrical adaptation of the book *Uncle Tom's Cabin*. Even though slavery was on the decline in Maryland, interpretations of the book would highlight Baltimore's strong southern cultural presence.

When an antislavery newspaper in Washington paid abolitionist Harriet Beecher Stowe to write a serialized story highlighting the evils of slavery, no one knew it would become a sensation. Collected in book form in 1852, three hundred thousand copies were sold in America, and over one million were sold in England. It is impossible to overstate the polarizing effect it had on the American people. On one side, it was a morality tale depicting a corrupt, inhumane practice. On the other, it was a slanderous attack on an entire way of life—even reading it could be considered an act of insurrection. A Black freeman in Dorchester County, Maryland, named Samuel Green was convicted of a felony and given ten years in prison for just having the book in his possession.

That same year, Asa Hutchinson, a popular temperance singer, requested Stowe's permission to create a dramatization of her book. The deeply religious author would have none of it (it was theater, after all), but since the huge popularity of Stowe's novel would guarantee good business, the stage was fated to play a part in the slavery debate.

On January 5, 1852, the Baltimore Museum offered *Uncle Tom's Cabin; or, Life In the South As It Is*, supposedly written by "Mrs. Harriet Screecher Blow." This comic play is now lost, but based on published excerpts, its true author, Joseph M. Field, tried to shift to pathos in the final scene.[26] In Field's version, when Uncle Tom finally escapes to Canada and discovers its freezing cold winter, he sings "Carry Me Back to Old Virginny." When an abolitionist hears him and asks Tom what he wants, the Black man tearfully declares that he yearns to go back to his life as an enslaved man, and the play ends with "a gang of plantation negroes dancing 'Juba' and singing 'Old Jawbone.'" Months later, a touring production of another adaptation was shown at the Charles Street Theatre at least twice. It was written and produced by J.A. Keenan and also played in Alexandria and Washington, D.C. Instead of a satire, it was reported to be a "great moral drama" titled *True Southern Life or, Uncle Tom as He Is* and was intended for "all who wish to see the falsehoods of Mrs. Stowe exposed, and the institutions of the south sustained."

In 1855, John E. Owens returned to Baltimore to lease the Charles Street Theatre. He had purchased a farm in the village of Towsontown (later Towson), but it was not lucrative: "I tell you that were it not for John Owens the actor," he said, "John Owens the farmer would starve." Hearing of a version of *Uncle Tom's Cabin* by George L. Aiken that had been a big hit in

New York, Owens wrote the playwright to find out if it could be "softened" for a Baltimore audience and if "very objectionable speeches and situations could be modified."

Despite being a southern sympathizer, Owens seemed more concerned with not offending his audience than outright disputing Stowe's negative characterization of slavery. He may have heard that in the North, the play was drawing in a new demographic: church members who previously would not have been seen in a theater without embarrassment. When Owens mounted the edited version, it was a triumph, and his performance of Uncle Tom was praised. Houses were packed for five weeks, which saved his struggling season and put him on the road to becoming a wealthy man.

Ironically, it would be Jarrett, not Owens, who would find his southern audience's breaking point. After leaving the museum, Jarrett returned to Baltimore in 1859 with his own touring production of *Uncle Tom's Cabin*. It had previously played in Philadelphia, where it made $27,000 in two weeks, but apparently, it was so faithful to the book that an angry Baltimore audience drove the actors from the stage and destroyed the scenery.

The next occupant of the Baltimore Museum was George Kunkel, who renamed it Kunkel's Ethiopian Opera House. He was a basso-profundo singer and accordion player who left a job in a Philadelphia print shop to spend his entire professional life in minstrel shows. With companies such as the Virginia Serenaders and, later, his own company, Kunkel's Nightingales, he had already played every venue in Baltimore throughout the late 1840s and 1850s. Kunkel's strident southern viewpoint was made clear through the songs performed by the Nightingales. One written specifically for the company was "Aunt Harriet Becha Stowe." This story song follows a formerly enslaved man who goes to New York to find an absent Stowe. Unable to find work or food, the man decides to go back to "Virginny" to find his kind master.

It is interesting to note that, years ago, when Kunkel's Nightingales played at the Holliday Street, an advertisement was published inviting Black men to the third tier of the gallery to watch them perform. It is unknown how many free Black men came to watch his minstrel shows, but there is evidence that blackface was not universally accepted as a convention. The prominent abolitionist Frederick Douglass, who was bound into slavery and escaped from Baltimore's Fell's Point in 1838, called its practitioners "the filthy scum of white society, who have stolen from us a complexion denied them by nature, in which to make money, and pander to the corrupt taste of their white fellow citizens."

Nightingale Serenaders in blackface (detail). *From* Songs of the Nightingale Serenaders *(Philadelphia, PA: A. Fiot, 1846).*

Kunkel would go on to play the role of Uncle Tom many times in his career. In an interview, he later recalled presenting Aiken's five-act version of the play in Baltimore, but there is no record of these performances or their reception. In 1861, he revised the play in Charleston, but the city council, wishing to avoid the "corruption" of its Black citizens, passed a resolution forbidding any of them from entering the theater. Kunkel played the elderly enslaved man into his sixties, but these later productions were more likely "Tom Shows" or "Tommers," hundreds of productions that used the play version as a loose framework for inserting minstrel song and dance numbers, spectacle, live animals and, in many cases, scenes of happy plantation life. Changed by southern attitudes or used as an excuse for theatrical pageantry, Stowe's narrative came to serve any agenda, even on an international level. As far away as Brussels, the translation of the book changed the reason for the whipping of Uncle Tom to his believing in the immaculate conception.

The Booths

Today, John Wilkes Booth is probably the only nineteenth-century American actor that the average person can name due to his role as a presidential assassin, not his legacy of stage work. Yet he was a part of a very important but troubled American theatrical family that had ties to all of the theaters in Baltimore. Their story begins in 1821 with English actor Junius Brutus Booth headed for America, looking for a fresh start. The public story was that he had left England because he was tired of the constant competition with Edmund Kean and wanted his own fame and fortune. That may have been true, but biographers have also pointed out a more scandalous reason; the twenty-five-year-old had abandoned his wife and son for Mary Ann Holmes, an attractive dark-haired flower seller.

Junius Brutus Booth debuted in Richmond playing Richard III, and after years of touring, he became an established celebrity. While playing at the Holliday Street Theatre, he bought a farm near Bel Air, an isolated but attractive tract of land. Leaving Mary at the farm, he continued to tour, and in 1830, he tried his hand at managing both the Adelphi and Holliday Street Theatres. The venture was not lucrative, and after two years, he tried to break his lease at the Adelphi. In a letter to John Findlay, he stated the reason for his departure was "a severe illness which has rendered me incapable of attending to my affairs."

Only four of the Booth's nine children survived into adulthood, and three became actors: Junius Jr., Edwin (named after his friend Edwin Forrest) and John Wilkes. By every account, their childhood on the farm, with its forests, streams and bowers of flowing vines, was idyllic. In order to have a base to continue his theater career, the elder Booth bought a modest house on Exeter Street, only blocks from the Front Street Theatre, and the boys were sent to a finishing school and a private academy. Much to his father's disapproval, Edwin preferred drama to sports and created a theatrical club with John Wilkes and other neighborhood boys. They performed in the cellar of a hotel and charged one cent for children and two cents for adults. The scripts were shortened, and all women parts were cut. They even had a performance at the Adelphi, which was sometimes used by amateurs. The oldest, Junius Jr., was the first to strike out on his own to start an acting career, but he would later be overshadowed by his younger brothers for very different reasons.

Junius Brutus Booth was generally described by his contemporaries as gentle, courteous and generous. He was a vegetarian and insisted that no animals should be slaughtered on the farm and no trees should see an axe. One fellow actor recalled that when he accompanied Booth to an oyster room, every time a shell was forced open, Booth cried out "Murder!" in different tones. Stories about him also suggest a quirky sense of humor. He was known to bring a wagon full of vegetables to Baltimore to sell before a show. One day, he sold his produce and then went to a saloon at a local hotel that other farmers liked to frequent. Not recognizing him, one of the farmers suggested they all go to see Booth play Richard III. While they were getting tickets, Booth slipped around to the private entrance, changed into costume and performed the play. Afterward, he slipped back into his farmer's clothes and met the men back at the bar. Still not making the connection, a farmer asked if he liked Booth's performance. Booth told them that he could have played it better, a suggestion that generated laughter from the group.

Another aspect of his personality was described by others as a periodic melancholy or a "stormy passion," which was often exacerbated by heavy drinking. Alcohol abuse ran in the family. When Booth's father was invited from England to manage the farm during his absences, Booth wrote a letter begging him to give up "that destructive and Sense-depriving Custom of getting intoxicated," but he could not follow his own advice.

The actor's behavior was easy fodder for newspaper stories that praised his genius as a performer while gleefully writing of his "eccentric" exploits. It was reported that he once "pawned" himself to a companion for a drink and then put himself in the window of a pawn shop with a tag. Other stories were not so whimsical. When the actor was playing Othello, the moment when Othello smothers Desdemona with a pillow turned ugly when Booth bore down so hard that other actors had to come onstage and pull him off. His family never knew when a message would come from a distraught theater manager looking for their missing star actor. A few times, Booth even disappeared during a performance.

Later, a teenage Edwin became his father's guardian when he was on tour, because it was believed that he had a calming effect on him and could temper his drinking. As much as Edwin loved and admired his father, it must have been very difficult to be his caretaker. While the elder Booth was in New York and engaged to play Richard III, he descended into one of his moods and simply refused to go on. When Edwin tried to convince him, his father bluntly replied, "Go act it yourself." Pressured by the stage manager, Edwin put on his father's costume and performed the part for a surprised but ultimately pleased audience. During his eventual career as an actor, Edwin would go on to play many of his father's roles.

Junius Brutus Booth and his son Edwin. *From the Folger Shakespeare Library Digital Image Collection.*

While touring in California, the men's living conditions were so bad that the elder Booth decided to head back East but insisted that Edwin stay behind for "valuable experience." Penniless, Edwin wandered for days through sawmill camps until he reached San Francisco and landed some acting jobs. When his father died in 1852, it seemed to trigger Edwin's latent alcoholism. He began a romance with Laura Keene and traveled to Australia to perform with her, but during a drunken tirade at a hotel, he cursed the British government, and audiences stayed away. When he returned, he headed back to Baltimore to play Richard III at the Front Street Theatre.

The elder Booth had wanted John Wilkes to become a farmer, but the young man shared the same ambitions as his brothers. He tested the waters by playing one night at the Charles Street Theatre, but the number of hisses during the show kept him off the stage for two years. When he started again, he acted under the name "J.B. Wilkes" so as not to exploit his famous father's name. Unlike Edwin, who had spent considerable time watching and learning from his father on tour, John Wilkes was mostly self-taught, and

From left to right: John Wilkes (Marc Antony), Edwin (Brutus) and Junius Brutus Booth Jr. (Cassius) in *Julius Caesar*, 1864. *From the Brown Digital Repository, Brown University Library.*

it showed. When he finally decided to use the Booth name, his initial lack of skill probably embarrassed Edwin, who decided the country should be divided among the three brothers. Edwin would get the lucrative northern cities, Junius Jr. would have the West and John Wilkes would appear in southern theaters. As a result, John Wilkes spent the early part of his career in Virginia, where he acquired or solidified his pro-southern sympathies.

In 1864, Edwin, an abolitionist, voted for the first time in his life by casting a ballot for Abraham Lincoln. Days later, he arranged for all three Booth brothers to play *Julius Caesar* at the Winter Garden Theatre in New York, a benefit for a statue of Shakespeare to be erected in Central Park. This would be the first and last time all three brothers would act together. In the middle of the show, the police interrupted, looking for incendiary devices. Afterward, it was revealed that a Confederate plot to start fires all over the city had been discovered. When John Wilkes announced his support for the venture, Edwin angrily kicked him out of his house.

Although John Wilkes played Marc Antony in *Julius Caesar*, he identified with Brutus, Caesar's killer. After he shot Lincoln at Ford's Theatre in Washington, he jumped onto the stage wearing his father's costume spurs and yelled out, "*Sic Semper Tyrannis!*" Translated from Latin, the phrase means "Thus always to tyrants." Not only was it attributed to the historical Brutus, but it was also the state motto of Virginia. The shame of his brother's actions did not keep Edwin from the stage. He would go on to become one of the most celebrated actors of his generation, but he would always skip over Washington, D.C., to play Baltimore. Many commented on his aloofness and the fact that whenever someone mentioned his ill-famed brother, the brooding man would leave the room.

John T. Ford

Like John Wilkes Booth, John T. Ford is a person inextricably linked to the Lincoln assassination. What is overlooked is that he was one of the most important theater managers of his era. It could be argued that he heralded the end of the "actor-manager," who ruled both onstage and backstage. It would be businessmen, not stars, who would eventually become the driving force in the industry.

Ford was born in Baltimore in 1829, the second of seven children, and came from a lower middle-class family. His father was a shoemaker on Light Street, and Ford spent his early years watching performers like John E. Owens at the museum. He went to Virginia in 1847 to take a job as a clerk in his uncle's tobacco factory and spent the next two years going to the Richmond Theatre, where he watched figures like Macready, Forrest and the elder Booth and absorbed how a good theater should be run.

At seventeen, he married his sweetheart, Edith, who was the same age. Despite being tiny and frail, Edith, over the course of their marriage, bore Ford fourteen children, not counting the three who died in infancy. He was apparently a devoted husband and father, but as his family grew so did the pressure to support them. In an effort to make more money, he left the factory to open a newspaper agency and bookstore. It was close to the Richmond Theatre, and having plays in its inventory caused it to become a hangout for actors. Around this time, he built a relationship with minstrel performer George Kunkel. In 1849, Kunkel's six-person company toured through Richmond, and Ford wrote a play for them to perform, a burlesque called *Richmond As It Is*. It does not survive but was undoubtedly filled with local references. By the following year, Kunkel was so impressed with the young man that he asked him to be the assistant manager for the group, and when the manager retired from the business, Ford became the primary agent. Through this job, Ford learned to be the advance man for cities and towns they toured, wrote copy to publicize shows in local papers, sent editors potential news stories and acted as a house manager for performances. For the next four and a half years, he traveled all over the East, South, North and Midwest, gaining a thorough theatrical education. Along the way, he also gained a reputation for being a capable, polite and obliging gentleman, words that were used over and over to describe him.

The tours must have gone well, because in 1855, Ford joined with Kunkel and one other member of the Nightingales to lease three theaters: the Holliday Street Theatre, the Richmond Theatre and the National Theatre in Washington, D.C. Ford stayed behind to manage in Baltimore and handled the star bookings for all three venues. Until he took over, the Holliday had been doing poorly. For almost ten years, multiple managers failed to make a profit, and sometimes, the theater was dark for months.

Ford ran the theater for the next five years, and when the partnership dissolved, he became the sole manager. During that time, the Front Street Theatre and Baltimore Museum were his fiercest rivals. To compete, he began his seasons earlier and ended them later, and his was the only theater to have a fall/summer season. Ford believed in the star system—two-thirds of his first season had headlining performers, such as Forrest, Booth and Owens. He was also committed to developing the talent in his stock company so he would not be so reliant on stars. He trusted his actors to draw crowds, as evidenced by his leasing of the Baltimore Museum. Ford had them perform there while a "combination" company was booked at the Holliday. "Combinations" were touring companies or opera troupes that performed only one piece and usually did not require the use of the theater's contracted players.

One of the shows Ford produced was *The Poor of New York* (1857), a domestic melodrama by Irish playwright Dion Boucicault about a middle-class family struggling to survive after a financial crash. The practice was to "localize" the play when shown in other cities. Retitled *The Poor of Baltimore*, Ford featured painted scenery depicting landmarks such as Monument Square, Federal Heights, a Madison Street mansion interior and, of course, the Holliday Street Theatre. The play was topical, as the financial panic of 1857 was in full swing, commonly thought to have been caused by a real estate bubble and faulty banking policies. However, Ford's capable management kept the theater stable while others faltered.

Bookings that worked during this time of uncertainty included grand opera. Despite the imminence of the Civil War, Ford decided to gut the theater and renovate it to accommodate more opera performances. Architect W.H. Raisin created a beautiful lobby with tapestries and polished mirrors and a wide stairway that led to the balconies. Five hundred gas jets were installed for illumination, capacity was doubled to two thousand and the dome over the audience was replaced with a flat ceiling for better acoustics. The décor suggested an elevated artistic experience. Seated in the audience, you could see painted profiles of Shakespeare, Mozart and Raphael, as well as a stage curtain that depicted "Cupid taught by the Muses." When it reopened in 1859, Ford boasted it was now "one of the most spacious, elegant and convenient theatres in the country!" It was likely the expense of this bold modernization led to the dissolution of his partnership with Kunkel, who went on to manage the Front Street Theatre.

With the coming of the war, prospects for Ford looked bleak, but once the Northern military took control of Washington, the region stabilized. Ford saw the nation's capital as a great investment, since it was, as he put it, "packed with the various concourse attracted by a great army." He leased a former Baptist church and converted it into Ford's Athenaeum. Sadly, a fire caused by a defective gas meter ensured that it would operate for only one year. Out of kindness, another theater offered Ford a benefit to offset his losses, but Ford refused it for himself and gave the proceeds to his company members.

After gathering subscribers, he then built the now-legendary Ford's Theatre in Washington, D.C., whose façade was modeled after the Holliday Street Theatre. Ford understood he would have one famous guest seeking much-needed respite. In the upper right-hand section of the house was a box separated by a partition, which could be removed when the president's party came to the theater. Business was so good that Ford was prompted to build another venue, the Washington Theatre, in 1862 and went on to manage theaters in Philadelphia, Alexandria and Cumberland. Business was shaky during the first two years of the war,

John Thompson Ford, probably in the mid-1860s. *From the Library of Congress, Prints and Photographs Division, LC-DIG-ds-07258.*

but Ford did fairly well until John Wilkes Booth changed the course of history.

Before the war, Ford's political leanings can be surmised from his printed comments and choice of plays. For example, a playbill for *Rip Van Winkle* starring Joseph Jefferson imagined waking up "another Jefferson to see the land he left on the anniversary of the day of independence, he strove so hard to achieve, now convulsed, almost disunited, by northern aggression and fanaticism." After Lincoln won the election, Baltimore was one of the stops on his way to his inauguration in Washington, D.C. When the Pinkerton Detective Agency warned Lincoln of a possible assassination attempt, he traveled through the city in the dead of night. Critics of the president-elect were outraged by his secret ride and called him a coward. Two weeks later, Ford added an afterpiece titled *A Comic View of the Flight of Abraham*.

In April 1861, the first blood of the Civil War was spilled in Baltimore. Because train lines were not connected, Union soldiers had to travel across town from President Street Station to Camden Station. As they crossed, they were taunted by anti-Union crowds who then attempted to create a blockade on Pratt Street. Shots were fired, and when the riot was over, there were four Union soldiers killed, twelve civilians killed and dozens wounded. Once martial law was declared and thousands of Northern troops held sway over the city, Ford no longer expressed his dissent. In Baltimore, he held a concert for the benefit of the poor featuring a chanting of the Declaration of Independence, and he started producing plays with patriotic overtones. The play Ford produced that was probably most representative of his personal stance was Dion Boucicault's melodrama *The Octoroon* (1859). It revealed the absurdity of slavery by showing a woman who cannot marry her love because she is one-eighth Black, a secret that could put her in bondage. At the same time, the play is filled with sympathetic southern characters and a villainous Yankee who wishes to expose her. Both sides could buy a ticket and hold on to their beliefs.

Ford was in Richmond at the time of the assassination and immediately wrote to the newspapers of his innocence. He was arrested in Baltimore at his home and held for thirty-nine days without a formal hearing. Once released, he made every effort to prove his loyalty to the Union. He held a benefit for the Lincoln Memorial Fund and gave a framed engraving of the deceased president to every police station that sold a lot of tickets. As for Ford's Theatre in Washington, it was seized by the government. Many considered it indecorous to hear laughter at a place of national tragedy and wanted to prevent Ford from profiting off Lincoln's death. Finally, the government's decision was to buy the theater for $100,000 and utilize it for the War Department. Henceforth, Ford rarely saw shows in his remaining Washington theater. By the end of the war, he only controlled one theater, the Holliday Street, but decided to expand by leasing the Front Street Theatre as well. Ford used that theater only sporadically and lost money. In a letter, he wrote, "I have kept an 'elephant' for nearly four years."

A postwar economic recession from 1865 to 1870 meant meager profits for theater owners all over the United States. All complained of being overtaxed, since they had to pay a municipal tax, a federal license tax, a 6 percent property tax and a 2 percent tax on incomes whether their theaters were profitable or not. Nevertheless, once the economy stabilized and the population soared, Baltimore theater would enter a time of tremendous growth. New theaters and new theatrical empires would be created until the arrival of film changed the city forever.

4

THE POSTWAR BOOM

Baltimore theater experienced a watershed year in 1869. One reason was the first appearance of British burlesque performer Lydia Thompson and her troupe, which was accompanied by a great deal of hype. Her advanced publicity claimed that in Europe, her beauty led men to literally hold torches for her as she walked by. Another story claimed a lovelorn fan had shot himself. Whether this was true or not, she had just completed a triumphant forty-five-week run in New York and was ready to conquer the rest of the country.

Burlesque, a parody of a serious subject, was nothing new on the American stage; it had been around since the eighteenth century. Even recently, Laura Keene had presented several long-run shows in New York that made fun of plays at other theaters. However, something about Thompson's brash group of "British blonds" in flesh-colored tights and skirts led to both outsized crowds and a great deal of moral condemnation by the press. In retrospect, Thompson's material was rather tame. Her troupe performed plays written in a singsong rhyme scheme that satirized mythological subjects (*Ixion*) or well-known plays (*Sinbad the Sailor* and *Blue Beard*) and contained comic anachronisms. Thompson added topical references, puns, popular songs with new lyrics and dances, such as the jig, the hornpipe and the racy can-can.

Critics accused Thompson of "gross innuendo," but their outrage may say more about the accuser than the accused. The nineteenth-century woman was supposed to be demure and sexless; the only ones who were supposed to show their legs were the silent, romanticized and rather passive dancers found in ballet. Thompson put forth a much different image. By playing all of the primary male parts, she controlled the narrative and put women's bodies front and center. In doing so, she tore apart norms of modesty and introduced a radical redefinition of femininity.

This approach would find a welcome home in Baltimore. When Thompson appeared at the Holliday Street Theatre in September, there was no backlash from critics. She was praised as "the cleverest of all burlesque actresses," and her audiences got larger as the run continued. In fact, her popularity in the city never waned. She returned many times with new shows until 1889 and earned the title "the queen of burlesque."

Another reason 1869 was important was that it was the year of the first booking of the Georgia Minstrels, one of the first successful Black minstrel show troupes, at the Front Street Theatre. This fifteen-member group was organized in 1865 and later managed by Charles Callender, a white tavern owner who described himself as the act's "owner." By claiming that some members of the group were formerly enslaved people from Macon, Georgia, the group's selling point was authenticity; advertisements called

Lydia Thompson, 1890. *Courtesy of Ohio State University, Jerome Lawrence and Robert E. Lee Theatre Research Institute.*

them "the only legitimate representations of Southern Plantation Life" (or "Simon Pure"). When they began their run, it was announced that there would be "no distinction in regard to admission on account of color." Black audiences flocked to the theater, and in an interesting turn, benches were set apart for white people. The troupe became so well known that any group with "Georgia" in the name indicated a Black minstrel company. As difficult as it might be to understand the complexities of Black performers wearing blackface, it is important to recognize their stark lack of opportunities and the fact that white audiences insisted on the convention. Ultimately, minstrelsy offered an opportunity for Black performers to earn a living and to present a more positive image of Black culture than the buffoonery offered by white entertainers.

A broadside for the Original Georgia Minstrels. *From the Harvard Theatre Collection.*

This would not be the only development in blackface minstrelsy. As the number of professional minstrel companies began to diminish over time, blackface performance moved into the amateur sphere. Starting in the 1880s and going well into the twentieth century, holding a minstrel show became a very popular fundraiser for churches, clubs and civic organizations in Baltimore. It was also absorbed into another already-thriving genre: vaudeville.

Vaudeville (or "variety") is the presentation of a series of short unrelated acts. In Baltimore, the term had been in common use since the late 1830s, when the Baltimore Museum touted "Vaudevilles and other Musical Entertainments." An act in a vaudeville show could be anything—singing and dancing, juggling, an animal or circus act, a scene performed from a serious drama, a magic act, ventriloquism or any other talent that would interest an audience for ten to fifteen minutes. It was also a repository for ethnic stereotypes played out in comic monologues and skits. A vaudeville bill commonly included what was called an Italian, Dutch, Irish or Hebrew comedian. Individual entertainers would give it their own spin, but generally, an Italian character would be represented as hyperemotional, a Dutch (or German, a corruption of *Deutch*) was lazy and conservative, an Irishman was presented as a drunkard and Jews would be portrayed as devious or dishonest. In addition to these qualities, comedy would derive from these characters' stupidity or bad pronunciation of English words. When it came to the representation of Black people, white performers in blackface continued in vaudeville. Black performers had limited representation, and typically, only one act featuring a Black person was allowed in a vaudeville show.

The last noteworthy event of 1869 was the introduction of "high class vaudeville" by Maryland-born "Colonel" William E. Sinn. Sinn was a former traveling salesman who switched careers to join his brother-in-law in managing theaters in Washington, Alexandria, Cincinnati and Philadelphia. He never served in the Confederate army but was promised an honorary rank for helping enlist a Maryland regiment to fight for the

The Odeon Theatre, circa 1895. It was lost in the Great Fire of 1904. *From the Maryland Center for History and Culture.*

Southern cause. During the war, he was arrested at the Union border, taken to Baltimore and given the choice of taking the oath of allegiance or staying in Fort McHenry. Sinn took the oath but also claimed the Confederate title he felt he was owed.

When Sinn took control of the Front Street Theatre from Ford, he immediately changed its name to the Front Street Theatre Comique. Vaudeville had long had a reputation for being risqué and only suitable for male audiences, but Sinn must have discovered that profits doubled when clean variety acts were shown in New York. To reach this middle-class goldmine, he advertised ladies' matinees and encouraged them to bring their children, pointing out that the theater showed the same program at night, proof of its decency.

A year after this change, the Odeon Theatre opened on South Frederick and East Baltimore Streets as a beer saloon and concert hall for the German community. It was owned by local brewer Joseph Raiber, but it lasted only until 1871, when it was converted into the six-hundred-seat Odeon Theatre Comique. Unlike Sinn's venue, this early purveyor of vaudeville was considered a second-rate house. Its "big and only ten cent show" created a family matinee, but the pattern of women headliners, events such as "Roman and Grecian Statuary" and the inclusion of boxing and wrestling tournaments made its eventual move toward burlesque in the 1880s unsurprising.

The Curtain Rises and Falls

The post–Civil War era saw the creation of new theaters and the loss of ones that had been of great importance to the city. In 1864, the cornerstone was laid for the Concordia Opera House on the west side of Eutaw Street, south of German Street (now Redwood Street), also known as Concordia Hall. Designed by famed architect Adolf Cluss, it was financed by an organization of affluent German Jews, and when it was finished a year later, visitors marveled at the marble columns in the lobby and the theater's one thousand seats covered in red velvet, carpeted floors and large gilded chandeliers. This opulence was made possible by some cost-cutting; the seats were made by prisoners at the Maryland Penitentiary. The building also had a buffet, lunch and billiard room attached. For years, it showed German-language theater, as well as operas, concerts, lectures and readings by luminaries like Charles Dickens. The building was destroyed by fire in 1891.

The interior of the Concordia Opera House. *From* Die Gartenlaube, *1866, 77.*

After managing the Holliday Street Theatre for fifteen years, John T. Ford finally bought it in 1870 and decided to expand. A year later, he built Ford's Grand Opera House on Fayette Street between Howard and Eutaw Streets. Designed by James Gifford, it cost $175,000 and was remodeled in 1893. Three stories high, it had an 1,800-seat capacity, used electricity to light its gas fixtures and its stage and box office were connected by telegraph. It would be the premier venue for plays in Baltimore until the 1960s.

In 1873, Ford received a major setback. In September, Mrs. Linton, the person in charge of the wardrobe at the Holliday Street Theatre, was awakened by smoke at 2:30 a.m. She lived on the third story of the theater with her two children. When she investigated, she saw flames darting along the rigging and border curtains. She woke her children, and even though they were severely burned, they managed to escape through a window and drop to street level. Blistered but determined, Linton rushed to the wardrobe room to try to save the inventory but was forced to leave by firemen who were seeking to stop the blaze. Shortly after 3:00 a.m., the roof collapsed, and by 4:00 a.m., only the bare walls were left standing. Damage was also done to the St. Nicholas Hotel, where actors were housed; a mattress factory; and the City College (formerly the Baltimore Assembly Rooms). By morning, a photographic emporium was selling stereoscopic views of the ruins on

Right: Ford's Opera House, 1916. It booked shows intended for Broadway until the 1950s. It was demolished in 1964 to make way for a parking garage. *Author's collection.*

Below: The seating plan of Ford's Opera House, 1888. *From Hutzler Bros. Baltimore Guide (Baltimore, MD: A. Hoen, 1890).*

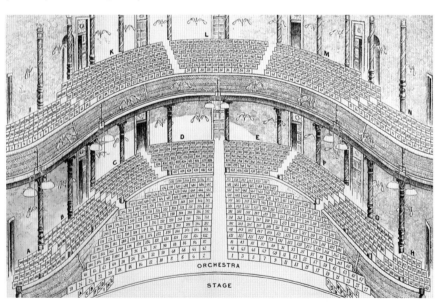

Holliday Street Theatre, circa 1906. The theater was torn down in 1917. *Author's collection.*

Holliday Street. A year later, the Holliday was rebuilt in the neoclassical style, and the years of its major changes were displayed at the top of its façade, a record of perseverance.

Also lost to fire that year was the Baltimore Museum, but it would not experience a rebirth. Time had not been kind to the venerable institution. It had not been a thriving concern for some time, much to the consternation of various managers. It would often have a flurry of activity and then sit empty. Over time, it started to be considered more of a saloon than a theater, and when it was occupied for a dance in 1866, a man was shot, which worsened its reputation. Three years later, a travel guidebook declared that the museum only "serves to gratify the juvenile dramatic taste." On December 12, 1873, the museum hosted a dance under its new name, the New American Theatre, and in the middle of the night, a fire on the fourth floor burned its way down to the street. During the half-hour conflagration, the walls became so unsafe that ladders could not be placed against them to fight the fire. Across from the theater was Barnum's Hotel, where fifty employees manned the roof with buckets of water to extinguish any embers that came their way. It was a total loss in the amount of $26,475 but was covered by insurance. The site was then sold to the Baltimore and Ohio Railroad Company for $225,000. Later,

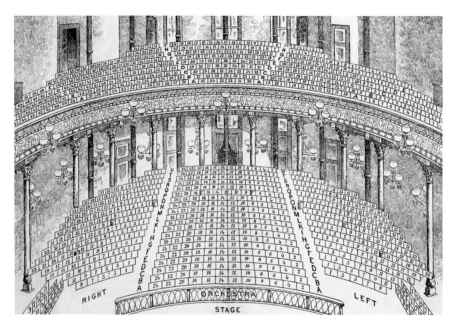

The seating plan of the Holliday Street Theatre, 1888. *From* Hutzler Bros. Baltimore Guide *(Baltimore, MD: A. Hoen, 1890).*

the Emerson Hotel was built on the site, but it was razed in 1971. Today, a bank occupies that corner.

The next theater that was lost also had a long history. In 1837, William C. Harris decided to purchase property on the south side of Baltimore Street east of the bridge, the site of an old tavern. He hired William Minifie, who was also responsible for designing the Front Street Theatre ten years earlier, to erect a four-story building called Washington Hall.[27] By the time it was completed, financial problems forced Harris to sell it for $20,000. In 1839, the new owner outfitted the space into a one-thousand-seat theater with a curtain depicting the Capitol Building. He renamed it the Vaudeville Pavilion, but subsequent advertising reveals it was rented only briefly for performances. For the next ten years, it reverted back to Washington Hall and was one of many places in the city that did a lively business of booking professional meetings, music clubs, panoramas, lectures, fairs and balls. In 1848, it was renamed the Olympic Theatre and was utilized as "a theatrical saloon." From 1860 to 1864, it became a vaudeville house called the Melodeon, and in 1865, it became the New Casino. In 1867, its name was changed to the Baltimore Opera House, and it began to embrace the rising trend of burlesque, maintaining the questionable claim that it was the

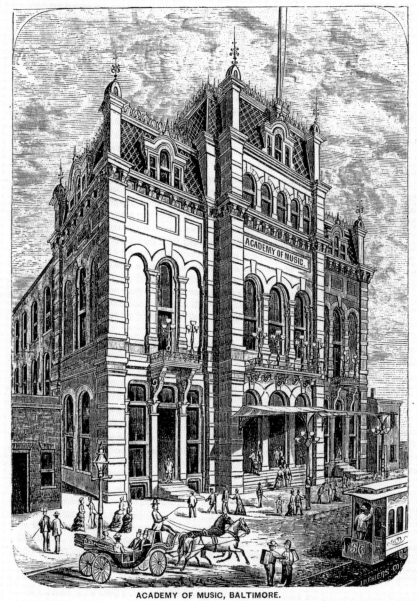

ACADEMY OF MUSIC, BALTIMORE.
(NORTH HOWARD STREET.)

The Academy of Music. *From George Washington Howard,* The Monumental City, Its Past History and Present Resources *(Baltimore, MD: J.D. Ehlers, 1873), 332.*

The Academy of Music holds a grand ball for the benefit of impoverished children. *From Frank Leslie's Illustrated Newspaper, April 24, 1880, 120.*

The Lyric Theatre, circa the 1910s. After the Concordia Opera House burned down, the Lyric was built in 1894 for concerts and operas. *Author's collection.*

place where the French can-can was "first produced on this continent." On October 13, 1874, a 2:00 a.m., fire completely destroyed the theater, as well as some adjoining retail stores. Actresses in a nearby boardinghouse had to be taken down to street level with fireman's ladders. One of the local papers dryly mentioned that all of the destroyed buildings were owned by the same person and heavily insured.

In January 1875, Ford's lock on Baltimore theater was broken by the creation of the Academy of Music on North Howard Street near Franklin Street. This beautifully adorned theater, with its gilded walls and large crystal chandelier, sat 1,800, with a smaller concert hall that could fit 1,400. It was a home for Italian operas, concerts and tableaux vivants (with Miltonian, biblical and mythological subjects), as well as lavish balls with dancing and champagne. It also hosted charitable organizations that organized events like the Martha Washington Tea Party, where the wealthy would carouse in colonial garb and powdered wigs. Under later management, the theater showed vaudeville and touring shows.

The city would also say goodbye to the Adelphi in 1876. The theater had always struggled to find a lasting audience, and as early as 1832, there was a mention that it was "now but rarely open." Five years later, a directory listing said it was occasionally used for the exhibitions of paintings. In 1840, the name of the theater was changed to the National Theatre, but it was open for only a brief period. New management closed the bar in 1842 so it could promise "good order"—never a good sign. As it passed hands, it was also known as the Belvidere, National, Baltimore City and German City Theatre. In the end, it was used as a bazaar and, finally, a horse stable before it went up in flames.

THE IMPRESARIOS:
KELLY, FOREPAUGH, ALBAUGH AND KERNAN

There was a boom in Baltimore theater in the 1880s and 1890s, driven by a group of men whose reputations were so well established that their names were put in front of the venues they controlled. The first was Daniel A. Kelly. Born in New York, he was orphaned at the age of three and went to school until he was ten. He worked in a printing office, feeding a press, and for a time, he became a "pilot's boy," the assistant to a master mariner. He tried to travel west but ran out of money in Troy, New York, where he hired himself out steering boats on the canals. When the Civil War broke out, he enlisted as a drummer boy in the Union army. He then became a private in a New York regiment, part of the Army of the Potomac, and saw serious action. During one winter, the members of his company formed a theatrical troupe, and Kelly was their comedian. When the war was over, he ran into a friend from those days who was now member of the Bowery Theatre, and a position was secured for him. After his apprenticeship, he joined tours and was considered a strong "dialect actor" and comedian. He came to Baltimore as part of a sketch team with another Irishman named Dan Collier and played at the Holliday for three years. In 1880, he leased the Front Street Theatre, but the theater had such a poor financial outlook that his partner withdrew. Before one show, all the backstage crew said they would go on strike if they were not paid. Kelly responded by showing them the receipts and expenses and said if he ever made any money, he would pay them. The crew liked his frankness and work ethic and decided to stick around. After a popular dog act filled seats and Kelly's coffers, the theater got on firmer financial footing and began to thrive.

For thirteen years, "Kelly's Front Street Theatre" featured sensational melodramas, along with variety acts. Kelly even authored several plays, including *The Shadow Detective*, which turned out to be a big moneymaker. This potboiler allowed him to show off his dialect skills, as he played an investigator who assumes comic disguises (Italian, Irish, Yankee and

Scottish) to solve the mystery of a missing woman. Kelly's play used a variation of an old Victorian plot device. At the play's crisis point, two locomotives traveling at full speed are about to collide while a man is tied to the railroad tracks. It was such a hit that three hundred people had to be turned away. Kelly ended up touring with the play and performed it over two thousand times.

After Kelly's departure, the Front Street Theatre was the site of the worst theater disaster in Baltimore history. On December 27, 1895, a touring New York Yiddish-language company had sold the theater to capacity. Just as they were about to start their show, *Alexander, the Crown Prince of Jerusalem* (1892), an odor of gas was detected. While trying to find the leak, a man in the gallery used a light to trace the gas line, which

Daniel A. Kelly. *From Charles Edward Ellis,* An Authentic History of the Benevolent and Protective Order of Elks *(Chicago, IL: Charles Edward Ellis, 1910), 181.*

ignited a loose connection. It was no more dangerous than a pilot light, but someone saw the flames and yelled, "Fire!" What made the situation worse was that someone turned off the gas, causing some of the auditorium to go dark, which turned fear into panic. A frantic stampede to the exit jammed doorways, and when people did manage to escape, many attempted to go back inside to get loved ones. Police and firemen on the scene responded by using clubs and pick handles to beat them back. The *Sun* described the horrific scene:

> *Women ran here and there, calling the names of their children, rending their garments and beating their breasts and calling out that the curse of God was upon them.... The police and fireman worked with difficulty and finally had to turn several streams of water on the crowd to get it sufficiently dispersed to enable them to bring out the injured and the dead. As each body was brought out the crowd would push up around it and almost tear it away from the police and firemen in the effort to see if it was that of a person known to those about.*

The final count recorded twenty-three had been trampled to death, and nearly one hundred had been injured. After the old theater sat empty for a number of years, inspectors condemned it and scheduled its demolition, but the Great Fire of 1904 did the job for them.

The next impresario came from the world of the circus. Adam Forepaugh was one of the most successful circus managers of all time and the only serious rival of P.T. Barnum in scope and reputation. A consummate showman, he always believed bigger was better and spent most of his life entertaining audiences with performing animals, enormous menageries, stunt riders, jugglers, acrobats and clowns. An important part of his show was his traveling "museum," a space he created or rented in each town that he filled with "curiosities—living or otherwise," such as flute players, a "sleeping beauty," a "dancing negro," mechanical singing birds (long before Disney) and life-size wax figures of famous individuals, like Abraham Lincoln signing the Emancipation Proclamation.

To apply a veneer of educational value to the proceedings, historical events were staged in the ring. For example, equestrians became Pony Express riders, and chariot races became "Sports of the Roman Amphitheater." More violent spectacles were also provided, including recreations of Custer's defeat at Little Big Horn and the "Atrocious Mountain Meadow Massacre," the 1850 slaughter of settlers by Paiute Natives and Mormons dressed as Paiutes.

Forepaugh wanted to compete with Buffalo Bill's wildly popular show and became the first to incorporate a Wild West show into a circus, a problematic accomplishment. While it is true that these shows gave employment to Natives who lived on reservations with meager resources, they often did not represent their true tribe in these "historical" recreations, and there were rumors that Native performers were mistreated.

Wild West shows like Forepaugh's played a big role in shaping how Natives were perceived by white people. For the vast majority of Americans, their only encounters with Natives were wooden statues that decorated the outside of tobacco shops. At a Wild West show, they could see and admire a Native performer's skills but were also exposed to the crude stereotype of the "savage Indian" that had been perpetuated since the eighteenth century.

The first record of the Forepaugh circus coming to Baltimore is from 1867, when it performed at the Belair Market or Belair Lot (now at the corner of Forrest and Orleans Streets), a location used by many other circus companies. After multiple tours, the vast crowds and rave reviews must have inspired John A. Forepaugh, Adam's adventurous nephew, to find a permanent place in Baltimore to show "legitimate theater." This term had been used since the 1850s to separate plays from other theatrical forms, such as vaudeville and burlesque.

John grew up in the family business. At the age of six, he was a circus rider but had to leave to attend school. At twelve, he rode for a circus in Philadelphia, and at sixteen, his uncle gave him the responsibility of managing his own show. By the time of his uncle's death, John had moved away from the circus and had become the proprietor of Philadelphia's Broad Street Casino and the Forepaugh Theatre, which was named for him. His next venture was to lease the theater inside Baltimore's Grand Masonic Temple on Charles Street.

The temple was designed by architect Edmund G. Lind, who also designed the Peabody Institute and Baltimore City College. The cornerstone was laid in 1866, and the building cost $450,000 to complete. It was three stories tall and made of pure white marble. Engraved in the pediment, the triangular gable that connects to the roof, was one of the Masons' most important symbols, the "all-seeing eye" or "Eye of Providence." The first floor contained the Corinthian Hall, a lecture space that could accommodate 500 people and was available for a $30 rental. The second floor contained a large Main Hall that could be rented for $75 per night and fit 1,658 people. The third story was reserved for fraternity business. Although it is not entirely clear from period documents, the second floor probably comprised the Temple Theatre and was likely set up with a raised stage with ropes and pulleys for curtains.

For a time, the theater had been leased by a Patrick Harris and was known as Harris's Museum. Apparently, Harris did not enjoy a stellar reputation— the *Baltimore Sun* called him "a manager of cheap amusements." Forepaugh outbid him and agreed to pay $10,000 a year, along with $5,000 dedicated to improvements. This was too rich for Harris, who moved on to manage the Academy of Music.

After months of renovation, a notice appeared that said the new Temple Theatre promised to provide "three hours of wholesome Amusement" and could be considered "A Place to Take Your Wife. A Place to Take Your Children. A Place to Take Your Sweetheart." The theater reopened on October 17, 1887, with the play *Saints and Sinners*, by Henry Arthur Jones, a play about "Modern English Middle-Class Life." At the Temple Theatre, there was a new play presented each week, a mix of current productions, such as *Pavements of Paris*, and older, well-known melodramas like *Jane Eyre* and *Rip Van Winkle*. Ever the showman, Forepaugh illuminated all of Charles Street every night so that potential patrons would follow the lights directly to his theater.

On December 25, 1890, a fire started in the catwalk an hour before a performance and immediately set the curtains on fire. The building

Above: The Masonic Temple, circa 1906. *Author's collection.*

Opposite: The Grand, 2023 (formerly the Masonic Temple), rebuilt and expanded after fires in 1890 and 1908. *Photograph by the author.*

was gutted, and the subsequent remodel removed the theater in favor of exhibition spaces. There is no mention of further theatrical performances in the space after it was restored. The Masons moved to another building, and the temple became a federal courthouse. When a new courthouse was built, the building was used as an extension. In 1998, plans for the building to become a parking garage were stopped when it was sold to Tremont Suite

Hotels, which oversaw a complete restoration. Today, it is called the Grand, and its nineteen elegant ballrooms are used for meetings and events and as locations for the shooting of television shows like *Veep* and *House of Cards*.

The next important figure was John W. Albaugh, who had a long and highly successful career. He was born in Baltimore in 1837 and started acting when he was sixteen; his first role was Portia in an amateur production of *The Merchant of Venice*. His first professional appearance was at the Baltimore Museum under Jarrett and, later, the Holliday Street as a "walking gentleman." He went on to act with all of the prominent actors of the period, including Charles Kean, Edwin Booth and Edwin Forrest. It was thought that his Iago was the best in the country. His wife, Mary Lomax Mitchell, was also a noted actor, and the two played leading parts together after they were married. Albaugh eventually moved to management and built or leased theaters in Washington, D.C., as well as New York, Kentucky, Alabama and Canada. Albaugh added Ford's Holliday Street Theatre to his holdings in 1879.

Another theater in Baltimore became available to Albaugh due to a long-lasting party. In 1858, a popular musician named Otto Sutro decided he needed to make up for missed invitations from friends and held a birthday party for himself in his apartment on Charles Street. This high-class soirée was so successful that it was transformed into a social club that met every Wednesday and held amateur performances of music and drama. The "Wednesday Club" continued during the Civil War, despite the fact that social organizations had been banned, proof of the high social standing of its members. Keeping with the club's lighthearted atmosphere, the plays it mounted were mostly popular comedies and comic operas. The performances seemed to have been admired, especially the set dressing, which was augmented by wealthy members' home furnishings. With its roster growing and more space needed for its activities, the club moved to various locations until a building was purchased on North Charles Street (between Preston and Biddle Streets) in 1879. It was designed by George A. Frederick, whose commissions included Baltimore City Hall. The theater was on the first floor, and

JOHN ALBAUGH.

John Albaugh. *From T. Allston Brown*, History of the American Stage *(New York: Dick & Fitzgerald, 1870), 11.*

the clubhouse was on the second. When the club was disbanded in 1886, Albaugh saw that the city was growing north and west. Seeing a promising opportunity, he bought the theater at auction.

Now operating as "Albaugh's Lyceum Theatre," it would go through dramatic changes in 1890. Its interior was gutted and replaced, except for its side and back walls. When it was completed, it boasted steam heat, "superior ventilation" and electric lights, which were now being used in other theaters like the Holliday and Odeon. The press called it the most beautiful theater in Baltimore and "the equal of any house in the country." It opened on November 3, with two weeks of Shakespeare plays performed by Edwin Booth and Lawrence Barrett. The fact that audiences came to see Booth play Hamlet at the age of fifty-seven shows how willing they were to suspend their disbelief in order to see a famous actor play one of his signature roles. Over ten years, Albaugh presented mostly domestic melodramas. Based on the number of educational lectures he offered at the theater and newspaper caricatures depicting him in a top hat, monocle and striped pants, his theater seemed to have a highbrow reputation.

After twelve years, Albaugh sold the theater to Plimpton Chase, a Washington lawyer and theater manager, who switched to what he called "polite vaudeville." Chase promised that "there shall never be a word spoken or a situation offered on the stage that would offend the sensibilities of the most refined lady." The theater changed hands two more times before it was bought in 1920 by a company founded by James Lawrence "Addie" Kernan, considered the greatest of all Baltimore theater men.

Kernan also grew up in Baltimore; his father was a feed store owner on Front Street. Around the time he was a student at Loyola College, he boarded with the Booth family and befriended John Wilkes. After completing his education at Mount St. Mary's College, he worked with his father and then as a clerk in the transportation department of the Baltimore and Ohio Railroad. When the Civil War broke out, the twenty-three-year-old enlisted in the Confederate army. When he was captured, he was taken to Point Lookout Military Prison. Unlike Sinn, when given the option to sign an oath of allegiance to the Union and go home or stay in prison until the end of the war, Kernan chose the latter.

In 1866, his older brother became an investor in what became the Baltimore Opera House. When the lessee defaulted on a loan, James was put in charge of the risky enterprise. The theater was not held in high esteem, and the area near the Jones Falls Bridge had a poor reputation due to crime. After a few years, the theater burned down, but James raised enough money

Above: The interior of Albaugh's Lyceum. *From George W. Engelhardt,* Baltimore City, Maryland *(Baltimore, MD: Board of Trade of Baltimore City, 1895), 34.*

Left: Albaugh's Theatre program, 1905. *Author's collection.*

Opposite: James L. Kernan. *From the* National Police Gazette, *May 19, 1883, 4.*

JAMES L. KERNAN,
THE BALTIMORE THEATRE MANAGER.

to rebuild it on the same site. The New Central Theatre opened on August 16, 1875, as a vaudeville house, and it became the Monumental Theatre after a remodel in 1880. Commonly called "The Bridge," it was three stories tall and had seating for 1,700. There were also two galleries, roomy private boxes and a curtain depicting the Washington Monument. It also included a barroom and billiard parlor. Kernan was a showman and would do anything for a crowd. He also operated a summer garden next door with nightly concerts, pool tables, bowling alleys, a shooting gallery, "a woman diver," a boxing ring for the "fistic arts" and a bicycle track for races. He also ran a skating rink, free for theater patrons. Just like they did at other theaters, the house band played outside to drum up business.

By the 1890s, Kernan had devoted the Monumental entirely to burlesque. Two of the companies he booked are clear examples of how much burlesque had moved away from the woman-centric days of Lydia Thompson. The first was the Little Egypt Burlesque Company. Little Egypt was the professional name of a French Canadian belly dancer named Ashea Wabe. In 1896, she made front-page news for her connection to a stag party for a wealthy socialite named Clinton Seeley, one of P.T. Barnum's grandsons. It was held at Sherry's, one of the posh marbled restaurants used by "the four hundred," elite members of New York high society. The police were given a tip that Little Egypt, one of the performers for the evening, was going to dance in the nude—or in Wabe's words, "give them something to take home with them." A police captain took it upon himself to bring several officers to the restaurant in order to arrest her. Much to the consternation of the guests, he stormed into the dressing rooms but could not find Wabe, because she was in a private room on another floor. After the police left, she danced for the men in a private room but did not dance "in the altogether," because her manager said there was trouble earlier in the evening. Seeley was outraged at the invasion of privacy and used his influence to get the captain put before a police board. The event became known as that "awful Seeley dinner," and it gave his guests unwelcome national headlines by casting a light on the illicit activities of the male well-to-do. According to Wabe, a man came to her door offering her $1,000 to leave the state, but she refused. Instead, she

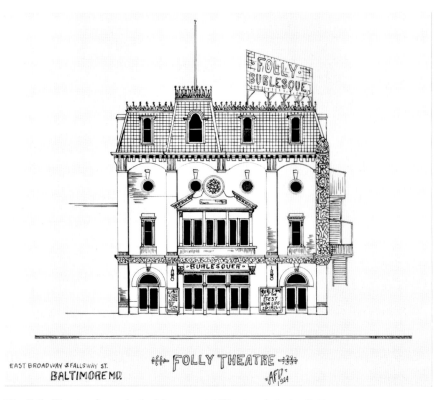

EAST BROADWAY & FALLSWAY ST.
BALTIMORE MD.

⟨⟨⟨ FOLLY THEATRE ⟩⟩⟩

·AFD·
1924

The Folly Theatre, formerly the Monumental Theatre. *Author's collection.*

immediately took advantage of the publicity by becoming the headliner of a touring burlesque company that not only recreated "the dances, scenes, and situations of the dinner" but also concluded with "a merry burlesque called 'Egypt in Court.'" Legend has it that the police stopped the Baltimore performance of the show. The second sign of how burlesque was changing was the Rose Hill English Folly Company, which featured a "disrobe act." Under the pretext of going to bed or changing to swim, a woman would appear as a shapely shadow behind a translucent screen. Voyeurism was becoming a defining feature of the art form.

In 1890, Kernan took over the high-class Holliday Street and changed its offerings to low-priced melodrama. That same year, he bought a building on Howard Street called the Natatorium and Institution for Physical Culture. Built in 1870, it housed an indoor pool, swimming academy and barbershop. Kernan remodeled it into the Auditorium Theatre, mostly a vaudeville house, with a lobby that featured a "palm garden" and tableaux made of automatons. One called "The Death of the Gamekeeper" depicted a dying

The Rose Hill English Folly Company, 1899. *From the Library of Congress, Prints and Photographs Division.*

man's chest rising and falling while the gears produced a wheezing sound. Popular actors who appeared there included Weber and Fields, Tony Pastor, Alice Fischer and Vesta Tilley.

After the turn of the century, Kernan's ambitions were still unsatisfied, so he decided to embark on what he called his "million dollar triple enterprise" on the corner of Howard and Franklin Streets. In doing so, he created the first theater district in the city. Kernan had the Auditorium Theatre rebuilt but kept the swimming pool, now part of a Turkish bath purported to cost $50,000. He also erected another theater called the Maryland on the former site of his father's store. Combined, there were 3,732 seats. Between the theaters was the Hotel Kernan, which had an art gallery, mahogany furnishings, brass beds, a dining room and a rathskeller with a seventy-two-foot-long Italian marble bar, the longest in Baltimore.[28] The entire complex had four electric generators, considered an attraction in itself, which lit up six thousand lights that were controlled by "white-clad machinists and uniformed attendants." After two and a half years of construction, "Kernan's Corner" opened on September 4, 1905.

The Maryland Theatre showed vaudeville, but Kernan, although a great entrepreneur, was not a great judge of talent. He often booked second-rate acts until he broke his leg on a slippery floor. While he was recuperating, he allowed his assistant to do the hiring who proved that better, more expensive acts resulted in better box office. The Auditorium mostly presented plays and musical comedies and would go on to showcase talents such as Mae West, Fanny Brice, the Marx Brothers, Sophie Tucker, Katharine Cornell, Helen Hayes, Ethel and Lionel Barrymore, Sarah Bernhardt and Spencer Tracy. Kernan also took over three theaters in Washington, D.C., and four in Buffalo. When he died in his hotel in 1912, his body was put on public view in the art gallery of the hotel, and thousands came to pay their respects. In his will, Kernan bequeathed controlling stock of his company to his favorite charity, the Hospital for Crippled Children, housed in a country mansion he had donated earlier.

Charles Edward Blaney was another influential Baltimore producer during this era and the only one to also gain fame as a playwright. Called "the King of Melodrama," his formula was simple: pull ideas from newspaper stories and local happenings and allow the audience to "delight in heroic heroes, winsome heroines, realistic villains and a gloriously happy end." When it came to plot, Blaney insisted his audience wanted "a series of vivid pictures flashed before them in rapid succession." By the end of his career, he had made a fortune by writing over one hundred melodramas and lighthearted comedies, with such

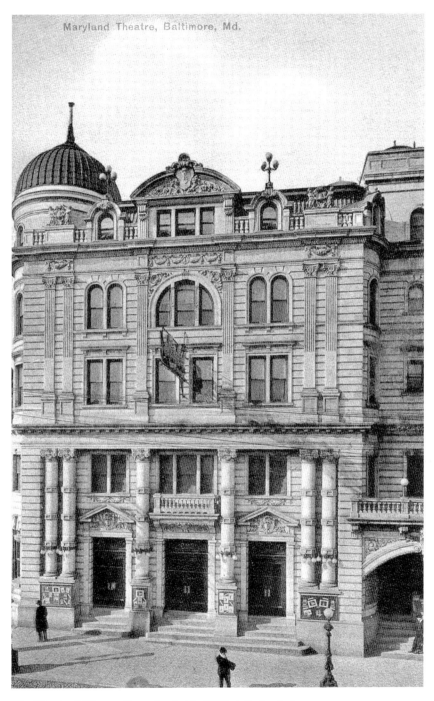

Maryland Theatre, Baltimore, Md.

The Maryland Theatre. It was leveled in 1948. *Author's collection.*

37-Auditorium Theatre, Baltimore, Md.

We will go to this Theatre next week. C. L. S.

Howard and Franklin Sts., Theatrical District, Baltimore, Md.

Opposite: The Auditorium Theatre, 1906. *Author's Collection.*

This page, top: Kernan's Corner before 1927. Kernan owned (*left to right*) the Maryland Theatre, Hotel Kernan and the Auditorium Theatre. *Author's collection.*

This page, bottom: Kernan's Corner, 2023. Remaining are Kernan's hotel (now an apartment building) and the façade of the Auditorium (later the Mayfair). *Photograph by the author.*

titles as *King of the Opium Ring* (1899), *The Factory Girl* (1903) and *Kidnapped for Revenge* (1907). He mainly wrote plays for a chain of theaters, but he also owned theaters in Newark, New Jersey, and Philadelphia.

In Baltimore, Blaney had his eye on a property on North Eutaw Street between Saratoga and Mulberry Streets. It was an old church that had been converted into a 1,000-seat theater in 1903 called the Empire, a place for vaudeville. That same year, it was leased to a stock company, but its actor-manager was swimming in debt, so he set fire to the theater for the insurance and then panicked and fled the city. Once the theater was repaired, it was leased to another company and renamed the Oriole. Blaney bought it in 1904, expanded its capacity to 2,200 and changed its name to Blaney's. It opened with one of his own plays, *Child Slaves of New York* (1903), a detective story about a stolen child. The *Baltimore Sun* described it as "throbbing with snappy action, thrills, laughter and tears."

Blaney immediately had competition from a theater on East Baltimore Street between East and Lloyd Streets. This Romanesque, cavernous structure, built on the site of Thomas Wall's eighteenth-century theater, was

Blaney's Theatre. The house musicians played on the balcony to attract crowds. *Courtesy Enoch Pratt Free Library, Maryland's State Library Resource Center.*

built as a powerhouse for cable lines before the electric trolley took over. In 1903, it was turned into Convention Hall and was occupied by various stock companies until it became the Bijou and played melodramas to large audiences. However, tastes would begin to change in the next few years, and the melodrama's days were numbered. In 1906, Kernan took over the Bijou and changed it to a "family theatre." In 1909, Blaney saw the writing on the wall and switched his theater back to vaudeville.

H.L. Mencken and the Drama Beat

In 1901, twenty-one-year-old newspaperman Henry Louis Mencken had been struggling to be noticed at the *Baltimore Herald*. However, it was not long before his industrious work ethic and snappy prose style soon got him elevated from city hall stringer to Sunday editor and chief drama critic. For Mencken, this assignment placed him on familiar ground. His parents were theatergoers, and he had spent his teenage years haunting the city's playhouses. Only a year before his promotion, young Mencken was mentioned in the *Baltimore Sun* as an eyewitness to a tragic incident at the Olympia Theatre concert saloon on Gay Street. According to Mencken and a fellow reporter, an intoxicated patron had passed out and could not be revived. A patrolman was called to deal with the situation, but thinking the man in no danger, he left him to sleep it off. The unfortunate man died soon after, and a high-profile police inquest was launched. The patrolman refused to accept responsibility for the man's demise, citing the victim's earlier proclamation that he was "the champion whiskey drinker of the United States." A grand jury agreed with him but decided the man's death rested not with his own appetites but with "sitters." These were actresses who, in addition to their duties on stage, were also paid to persuade men to buy drinks for a commission, a violation of the law. According to the jury, the man's tragic end was directly connected to the "dissolute character" of the women.

Mencken threw himself into his new assignment as a drama critic with characteristic vigor. He partook of Saturday matinees, relished the view from the front row and sought what he called "peace and recuperation" at burlesque shows at the Odeon. It did not take him long to set himself in opposition to the older critics. When a new play opened, Mencken mocked the critics from New York, like William Winter, who would descend on Baltimore clad in opera cloaks and plug hats, looking like "melodrama

H.L. Mencken, 1904. *Courtesy Enoch Pratt Free Library/Maryland's State Library Resource Center.*

villains." He believed they foolishly rejected innovative work and judged plays solely on their morality.

An early influence on Mencken was Robert I. Carter, the managing editor of the *Baltimore Herald*, who trained the young reporter in the art of writing the theatrical notice. Carter warned against trafficking with actors, advice that Mencken took to heart by meeting only with playwrights, managers and press agents. When he was a younger man, Mencken appeared only once on a stage and had only two lines, both of which he forgot. This incident, however, did not make him sympathetic to what he called "the so-called art of acting." Although a look at his reviews proves that he was never remiss in showing great admiration for the leading actors of the day when their performance merited it, he was no fan of the profession. Later, he wrote, "Of all the classes of men, I dislike most those who make their livings by talking—actors, politicians, pedagogues, and so on. All of them participate in the shallow false pretenses of the actor who is their archetype." In a 1905 *Herald* piece titled "A Discourse on Actors," Mencken began by celebrating the decline of the star system, in which a "tragedian could appear in any old play, no matter how meretricious or trivial, and the public would flock to see him." Now, wrote Mencken, "the chief figure in the theatrical concerns of the moment is not an actor, but a dramatist. The day of the stage idol is passing. Even the provincial stock companies are losing their brigades of worshiping matinee girls."

This focus on the dramatist was the influence of Will A. Page, a former dramatic editor of the *Washington Post*, who, like many newspapermen of the day, was lured away to become a press agent for a Baltimore stock company. Page taught Mencken to take theater seriously and exposed him to the progressive drama of Henrik Ibsen and George Bernard Shaw. In fact, Mencken championed Ibsen's controversial play *Ghosts* in its 1902 Baltimore premiere over the objections of other critics. He also worked on the translation of two of Ibsen's plays and wrote lengthy introductions for each one. Mencken was so enamored of Shaw that in 1905, he wrote the first book of criticism about him to be published in the United States.

This new genre of realism, spearheaded by Ibsen, was slow to be totally adopted on the American stage. This 1909 review of *The Bachelor*, a comedy by the most popular playwright of this period, Clyde Fitch, is indicative of Mencken's impatience: "It shows all of the little touches of realism—the turns of pungent phrase and bits of homely business…and it shows, too, all the stretches of probability, the signs of hurried, careless workmanship, the dependence upon stock theatrical types, and the occasional bursts of banality which marked his every drama, the best as well as the worst." In another review, Mencken provided his own checklist of questions patrons should be asking when evaluating a play: "Does its action develop smoothly? Is its sequence of events logical? Is its dialogue such as one might expect its people to utter in real life? In brief, is it built in a workmanlike manner?" In his summary of the 1905 season, Mencken touted only two plays that passed his test: *Magda* and *The Fires of St. John*, both by Hermann Sudermann. At the time, Sudermann was at the forefront of the naturalist movement in Germany, a subset of realism that emphasized the influence of the environment.

Magda is the story of a woman who left home at the age of eighteen to escape a marriage arranged by her father, a rigid military man. After forging a successful career as a singer, she returns to her hometown as a celebrated artist. There, she reconnects with a lover from her past who jilted her and, unknown to him, fathered her child. Now a well-respected and feared member of the local government, he proposes marriage but demands, for appearance's sake, that she send her son away for an undetermined time so that he can be adopted. Magda refuses, but when her father finds out the truth, he threatens violence if she does not accept the proposal. Impervious to his threats, she declares her independence, which causes her father to die from a stroke. *The Fires of St. John* is a tamer work with a similar spirit of rebellion. Marie, an adopted child, secretly loves George, the fiancé of her sister. Out of gratitude to the family that took her in, she represses her feelings and works to fix up a happy home for the couple. Soon, she discovers that George has also harbored secret feelings but has to marry Marie's sister in order to repay a debt of honor for his family. Moved by the arrival of St. John's Night, a holiday with pagan undertones and a time when passions are aroused, George and Marie confess their love and spend the night together. The title refers to St. John's Night, a holiday with pagan undertones, a time when passions are aroused. However, the next morning, they must soberly face their situation. George decides to go through with his loveless marriage, while Marie casts off the yoke of gratitude that has kept her miserable for so long. The play ends with her leaving the house forever. In addition to approving the way these plays were constructed, it is likely Mencken was attracted to them because they have characters who rebel against restrictive norms of morality.

Mencken occasionally tried his hand at theatrical writing. In 1900, he wrote the lyrics for a traveling musical show. In 1912, he penned a one-act play titled *The Artist: A Drama Without Words*, which was later performed at the Little Theatre in Philadelphia; in 1919, he wrote a play called *Heliogabalus* with George Jean Nathan and tried to get it produced in Europe. Although he later dismissed the project as a lark, in a 1927 letter, he revealed an emotional investment in the project: "You touch me in a tender spot when you speak of that scene in H[eliogabalus]. I wrote it almost in sobs. It is astounding how sentimental a decaying man can be."

For almost ten years, Mencken wrote theatrical reviews for the *Herald* (and later for the *Sun*). By his own account, he quit the theater beat after writing twenty-three unfavorable reviews in a row. He then teamed up with established New York drama critic George Jean Nathan to launch the *Smart Set*, a popular culture magazine, in order to write about broader subjects. Many Mencken scholars assume that his disillusionment with theater and his move to "a criticism of ideas" began in the 1920s, but his early theatrical reviews suggest it began much earlier. During his time as a critic, he wrote with equal passion about musical comedy, comic opera, vaudeville and burlesque as he did about the plays of Ibsen, showing a willingness to accept a work on its own terms. However, it is clear that a steady diet of pre–World War I plays took its toll. For every Ibsen, Shaw or Sudermann, there was a host of creaky melodramas. If he were alive today, Mencken would probably feel vindicated by the fact that plays by Fitch and others like him are not revived. As he would write years later, he did not have lofty goals for the stage; all he wanted was "an honest play, honestly produced and honestly played."

THE RISE OF FILM

Most Baltimore residents have probably heard of the "bawdy block," the raunchy red-light district bordered by East Baltimore Street, with a history of strip clubs, organized crime, peep shows and pornographic bookshops. This area began to acquire its seedy reputation in the 1940s, but previously, the area was known as the home of one of the country's great burlesque houses, the Gayety Theatre.

The Gayety rose from the ashes two years after the Great Fire of 1904. Constructed in only eighty-seven days and adorned with ornamentation suggesting the female form, the theater was a testament to the belief that burlesque was yet to reach its heyday. The 1,600-seat theater had a rich red interior with three tiers of boxes, a large rathskeller in the basement and an asbestos curtain to prevent the spread of fire. The Gayety showed "clean" burlesque for middle- and working-class audiences organized by the Columbia

Gayety Theatre, 2023. The building is occupied by Larry Flynt's Hustler Club. *Photograph by the author.*

A man in front of the Gayety Theatre, circa the 1920s. *Author's collection.*

Amusement Company, a business organization that sent shows to various theaters (also called spokes on its "wheel"). Male working-class audiences preferred "hot" burlesque, which pushed the boundaries of displaying the female body. This type of burlesque was provided by the Monumental, which was on the Empire Circuit, a direct competitor of the Gayety. By the 1920s, the Gayety had abandoned parody, and its shows had devolved into comics performing monologues and skits between dancing showgirls. Eventually, stripteases became the primary draw. In decades to come, the theater would provide work for top comedians, such as Eddie Cantor, Abbott and Costello, Jackie Gleason, Phil Silvers, Milton Berle, Henny Youngman and Red Skelton, as well as striptease artists, such as Gypsy Rose Lee, Margie Hart, Georgia Southern, Ann Corio and Blaze Starr.

Despite the Gayety's popularity, it would be vaudeville, not burlesque, that would become the driving force of entertainment in Baltimore. Entrepreneurs rushed to build new theaters to profit from its increased popularity, but at the same time, the arrival of film would simultaneously change the market and live theater's supremacy. According to historian Robert Headley, the first regular film exhibitions occurred in 1904 at Kernan's Maryland Theatre. Two years later, the first movie theater opened across the street from the

A program cover from the New Monumental, 1908. *Author's collection.*

Gayety. By 1910, there were close to one hundred movie theaters operating in Baltimore. During this transitional (and somewhat experimental) era of silent film, some theaters even paid actors to stand behind the screen to voice the characters.

It soon became obvious that moving pictures were going to be more than a novelty, so, hedging their bets, investors built new theaters to

Lubin's Nickelodeon, circa 1910. *From the Library of Congress, Prints and Photographs Division, LC-USZ62-137479.*

accommodate both vaudeville and film. In 1908, Sigmund Lubin, an early movie mogul, opened Lubin's Nickelodeon on East Baltimore Street with an eye-opening façade featuring statues and ornate reliefs. Vaudeville played upstairs, and the basement was used for motion pictures and "illustrated songs" (slides accompanied by music). Other theaters showed films as part of a vaudeville performance.

Over time, silent films got longer, and the combination stopped working. At the same time, the low overhead and reduced logistical demands made film more attractive to investors. When the Victoria Theatre opened in 1908 next to the Gayety, it was intended to be a 1,500-seat vaudeville house, and it provided motion pictures as part of its first performance. In 1913, Charlie Chaplin appeared live at the Victoria in *A Night in an English Music Hall.* After a fire in 1922, it reopened as a movie house. The same happened to the New Theatre on West Lexington Street, which opened in 1910. It was committed to "continuous vaudeville," a term for shows that played all day, midmorning to late night, for customers who wanted to enter and leave whenever they pleased. Four years later, it showed only movies. Later venues followed the same pattern. The Empire Theatre (later, the Palace) opened on West Fayette Street in 1911 as a popular "clean" burlesque and

Left: The site of the Victoria Theatre, now Club Chez Joey, 2023. The narrow entrance led to the auditorium, which is now a parking lot. *Photograph by the author.*

Below: The Everyman Theatre (formerly the Empire), 2023. *Photograph by the author.*

Above: The Hippodrome. *Author's collection.*

Left: A series of ornamental masks that greet you when you enter the Hippodrome, 2023. *Photograph by the author.*

The former State Theatre on East Monument Street, 2023. Built in 1927 for vaudeville and film, it is now a bank. *Photograph by the author.*

vaudeville house, but by 1922, movies were introduced to the program. In 1914, the Lord Baltimore Theatre on West Baltimore Street and the Grand Theatre on South Conkling Street opened with a mix of vaudeville and movies but eventually phased out live performance.

The two biggest exceptions were the Hippodrome on North Eutaw Street, built in 1914, and the Garden Theatre, built the following year. With three thousand seats, the Hippodrome was the largest playhouse south of Philadelphia and showed movies and vaudeville until 1951. In doing so, it gave Baltimore audiences fond memories of performers like Gene Autry, Cab Calloway, Al Jolson, Jack Benny and Bob Hope. The Garden Theatre on West Lexington Street was designed by famous theater architect Thomas Lamb and cost nearly $1 million to build. Above the auditorium was a space for live performances, which lasted until the mid-1930s.

The first public presentation of a "talkie" occurred in 1913 at Albaugh's Theatre, which exhibited monologues, scenes from grand opera and vaudeville. The *Baltimore Sun* correctly called the new technology "epoch-making," an assertion proven by the speed at which stage material was converted into film. For example, in September 1927, George Jessel appeared

Schanze Theatre (now the Arch Social Club), 2023. It was opened as a 495-seat vaudeville/movie combination in 1912. The façade retains its two muses. *Photograph by George Mitchell.*

at Ford's in the play *The Jazz Singer*. By January, Vitaphone technology allowed Baltimore audiences to hear Al Jolson in the film version. By the end of the 1920s, three decades of similar acts booked by various circuits made vaudeville seem old-fashioned. While it declined and movie houses proliferated, live theater would continue but never be as central to the life of the city as it once was.

The Golden Age

So, when was Baltimore's golden age of theatre? If a golden age is a time of achievement and prosperity, there are many periods you could choose, but perhaps the question is more personal than historical. For newly arrived Eastern European Jews living in East Baltimore, they might say it began in the 1900s, when acting legends Jacob Adler and Boris Thomashefsky started touring and the Bijou became the Princess and showed Yiddish theater. Perhaps some might name the 1910s, when Jewish audiences could watch the Alliance Players, part of an educational organization, stage playwrights such as Sholem Aleichem and Peretz Hirschbein. Others could also say it began in the 1920s, when the Monumental on Baltimore Street became the Orpheum, a Yiddish theatre, and a young actor named Molly Picon brought Yiddish shows from New York.

For Black Baltimoreans, who spent their lives walking into theaters through side entrances and enduring restricted seating, they might agree that the golden age began in the 1910s, when Pennsylvania Avenue became

This 2015 photograph shows Hendler's Creamery, previously the Bijou. The structure was abandoned by developers and will soon be demolished. *Photograph by Eli Pousson.*

Paul Robeson and others protesting segregation at Ford's Theatre, 1948. *From the Maryland Center for History and Culture, Paul S. Henderson Photograph Collection.*

an entertainment center. There, you could find all-Black vaudeville at the New Lincoln Colored Theatre, featuring "a Chorus of Creole Beauties." They might also pick the 1920s, when locals could go to the Black-owned Douglass Theatre and see the Lafayette Players, an important dramatic stock company, or enjoy amusing musical reviews, such as *Follow Me*, with comedians Billy Higgins and Clifford Ross. They could also watch vaudeville at the Regent Theatre, which the *Afro-American* called "a legitimate playhouse where colored patrons would not be humiliated by the odious presence of... Mister James Crow." At the same theater, they could also see nationally famous all-Black musicals such as *Shuffle Along* (1921) and *Chocolate Dandies* (1924), with a sixteen-year-old Josephine Baker in the chorus.

In the end, the theater is a place where we look to be entertained and enlightened by stories that, hopefully, are told in a language that speaks to us all. I would encourage everyone to explore the work of today's Baltimore theaters to discover if we are living in another time of growth and artistic excellence. It would be a shame to miss out.

NOTES

1. There is some debate about whether Thomas Hallam was their father or one of the Hallam brothers.
2. When referring to plays, the first known year of production will be displayed in parentheses.
3. The prohibition against presenting theater on Sunday would last well into the twentieth century.
4. Hallam was called by some "a man of irascible humor," which may have had something to do with his increasingly problematic personal life. In 1787, he had a colonial protégé named Sarah Tuke, an attractive but raw recruit. Critics recognized that she was obviously a favorite of Hallam but thought little of her talent. Sadly, she took ill on the way to Baltimore and did not survive. When Hallam's wife passed away in 1792, he married Sarah's sister, Eliza, another member of the company. Their substantial age difference did not go unnoticed—neither did the fact that only four weeks passed between Hallam's wife's funeral and the wedding.
5. The name Holliday Street Theatre would not be commonly used until the 1830s.
6. At the time, there were two other theatrical circuits. The northern one, run by John Hodgkinson and William Dunlap, was based in New York and traveled to Connecticut, Rhode Island and Massachusetts. The southern circuit was run by John Solee in Charleston and toured through Virginia and North Carolina.

7. Baltimore-born Rogers served with Lafayette during the war and was instrumental in the defense of the Port of Baltimore in 1781. Later, his son sold part of his father's lands to the city to create Druid Hill Park.
8. This nickname was also a comparison to a famous English child actor named Master Betty, who was called "the Young Roscius."
9. A theater manager later claimed that due to the mania surrounding Payne, many high-priced tickets were bought with no intention of being used, presumably for bragging rights.
10. The reader is encouraged to read the passage with a British accent to hear the rhyming couplets.
11. Ricketts, like Pool, has also been credited with creating the "first American circus." However, since he was not the first equestrian entertainer in America nor an originator of the form, a better description would be that he was a significant importer of an already popular international entertainment trend in Europe. He can also be seen as a link in a long chain that would eventually lead to the far more elaborate circuses of Adam Forepaugh, the Ringling Brothers and P.T. Barnum.
12. Merry was likely the second woman theater manager. Mary Sully West ran a theater in Norfolk, Virginia, from 1799 to 1804, after her husband died.
13. In addition to the theater, Finlay went to great ends to increase foot traffic on his property. He turned part of it into the Pavilion Bath House, a reading room he named the Colonnade and an attached saloon (both open from 7:00 a.m. to 11:00 p.m.).
14. The first was Warren and Wood's Chestnut Street Theatre in Philadelphia, which adopted it a year earlier.
15. All three plays were set in foreign countries, Upper Alsace, Poland and Prussia, respectively. It was rare to find American locales in early melodrama.
16. By 1837, the Theatre and Circus began to be called the Front Street Theatre in print.
17. *Ethiopian* was a catch-all term for a Black person.
18. The use of the word *opera* by minstrel performers was tongue in cheek. It suggested the use of popular music.
19. The last permanent building in Baltimore constructed for circus performances was the Roman Amphitheatre on the southeast corner of North Calvert and Franklin Streets, which opened on October 26, 1846. Its architect was Richard Cary Long Sr., and it sat five thousand people. As the name implies, the structure was circular (one hundred feet in

diameter), with a ring that was fifty feet in diameter. Among the feats of horsemanship, there were some minstrel performances, but I could find no evidence that it presented plays. It burned down a year after it opened.

20. For information about Junius Brutus Booth, see chapter 3.

21. There was trouble outside the Theatre and Circus as well. Billboards for shows were destroyed to such an extent that a reward of twenty dollars was offered by the Theatre and Circus to catch the culprit.

22. In 1848, Baltimorean George H. Miles won Forrest's contest for his play *Mohammed, the Arabian Prophet*, written in iambic pentameter. Miles either ignored or rejected the Islamic tradition of prohibiting any physical depiction of the prophet.

23. Barnum's City Hotel, considered the finest establishment in Baltimore, was owned by David Barnum, not the famous circus magnate.

24. Owens discovered that it was possible to be too funny. When he played a benefit for himself at the Front Street, audiences roared with laughter when he tried to play the last act of *Richard III*, especially during Richard's death scene. Ever the pragmatist, Owens played to his strengths by converting all subsequent performances of the character into a parody.

25. The museum had been taken over by Joshua Silsbee, an actor who specialized in Yankee roles and Albert Hamm, a member of the Orpheum Family, a vocal music group.

26. There is another account that states the play was written by a Baltimorean named "Professor Hewett."

27. In addition to the Front Street Theatre and Washington Hall, Minifie designed two churches, a Presbyterian church (1844) on the corner of South Broadway and Gough Street (now Har Sinai Church of Christ) and a Methodist Episcopal church (1866) on South Broadway between Gough and Pratt Streets.

28. In the late 1970s and 80s, when the building was known as the Congress Hotel, it was a performance space for punk and alternative bands like the Talking Heads.

BIBLIOGRAPHY

BOOKS AND ARTICLES

Allen, Robert C. *Horrible Prettiness: Burlesque and American Culture*. Chapel Hill: University of North Carolina Press, 1991.

Archer, Stephen M. *Junius Brutus Booth: Theatrical Prometheus*. Carbondale: Southern Illinois University Press, 1992.

Bogar, Thomas A. *John E. Owens: Nineteenth Century American Actor and Manager*. Jefferson, NC: MacFarland, 2002.

Brainard, Charles Henry. *John Howard Payne: A Biographical Sketch of the Author of* Home, Sweet Home. Washington, D.C.: G.A. Coolidge, 1885.

Bryan, Vernanne. *Laura Keene: A British Actress on the American Stage, 1826–1873*. Jefferson, NC: McFarland, 1993.

Cahn, Julius. *Julius Cahn's Official Theatrical Guide*. New York: Julius Cahn, 1907.

Chapelle, Suzanne Ellery Greene. *Baltimore: An Illustrated History*. Sun Valley, CA: American Historical Press, 2000.

Cowell, Joe. *Thirty Years Passed Among the Players in England and America*. New York: Harper & Brothers, 1845.

Crawford, Mary Caroline. *The Romance of the American Theatre*. Boston: Little Brown, 1913.

Curry, Jane Kathleen. "Women in Nineteenth Century American Theatre Management." PhD diss., City University of New York, 1991.

Dennett, Andrea Stulman. *Weird and Wonderful: The Dime Museum in America.* New York: NYU Press, 1997.

Dorman, James H., Jr. *Theatre in the Ante-Bellum South, 1815–1861.* Chapel Hill: University of North Carolina Press, 1967.

Dowell, Peter, ed. *"Ich Kuss Die Hand": The Letters of H.L. Mencken to Gretchen Hood.* Tuscaloosa: University of Alabama Press, 1986.

Downer, Alan S., ed. *The Memoir of John Durang, American Actor, 1785–1816.* Pittsburgh, PA: University of Pittsburgh Press, 1966.

Dunlap, William. *History of the American Theatre.* Vol. 1. London: Richard Bentley, 1833.

———. *Memoirs of the Life of George Frederick Cooke.* New York: D. Longworth, 1813.

Engle, Ron, and Tice L. Miller, eds. *The American Stage: Social and Economic Issues from the Colonial Period to the Present.* New York: Cambridge University Press, 1993.

Fennell, James. *An Apology for the Life of James Fennell.* Philadelphia, PA: Moses Thomas, 1814.

Frey, Jacob. *Reminiscences of Baltimore.* Baltimore: Maryland Book Concern, 1893.

Gilje, Paul A. "The Baltimore Riots of 1812 and the Breakdown of the Anglo-American Mob Tradition." *Journal of Social History* 13, no. 4 (Summer 1980): 547–64.

Gresdna, Ann Doty. *The Career of Mrs. Anne Brunton Merry in the American Theatre.* Baton Rouge: Louisiana State University Press, 1971.

Hall, Edward H. *Appleton's Handbook of American Travel.* New York: D. Appleton, 1869.

Hemphill, Katie M. "Bawdy City: Commercial Sex, Capitalism, and Regulation in Nineteenth-Century Baltimore." PhD diss., Johns Hopkins University, 2014.

Hewitt, John Hill. *Shadows on the Wall; or, Glimpses of the Past.* New York: AMS Press, 1971.

Hill, West T., Jr. *The Theatre in Early Kentucky.* Lexington: University Press of Kentucky, 1971.

Houchin, John H. *Censorship of the American Theatre in the Twentieth Century.* Cambridge: Cambridge University Press, 2003.

Howard, George W. *The Monumental City, Its Past History and Present Resources.* Baltimore, MD: J.D. Ehlers, 1873.

Ireland, Joseph Norton. *The Kembles and Their Contemporaries.* Boston: L.C. Page, 1886.

Johnson, Claudia D. "That Guilty Third Tier: Prostitution in Nineteenth-Century American Theaters." *American Quarterly* 27, no. 5. (December 1975): 575–84.

Kauffman, Michael W. *American Brutus*. New York: Random House, 2004.

Knowles, Mark. *Tap Roots: The Early History of Tap Dancing*. Jefferson, NC: McFarland, 2002.

Leech, Margaret. *Reveille in Washington: 1860–1865*. Garden City, NY: Garden City Publishing, 2011.

Leman, Walter Moore. *Memories of an Old Actor*. San Francisco, CA: A. Roman, 1886.

Lhamon, W.T., Jr. *Jump Jim Crow: Lost Plays, Lyrics, and Street Prose of the First Atlantic Popular Culture*. Cambridge, MA: Harvard University Press, 2003.

Ludlow, Noah Miller. *Dramatic Life as I Found It*. St. Louis, MO: G.I. Jones, 1880.

Luquer, Thatcher, ed. *An Unconscious Autobiography: William Osborn Payne's Diary and Letters 1796–1804*. New York, 1938.

Maginnes, Arant. *Thomas Abthorpe Cooper: Father of the American Stage, 1775–1849*. Jefferson, NC: McFarland, 2004.

May, Alonso. *May's Dramatic Encyclopedia of Baltimore*. Microfilm, Maryland Center for History and Culture.

McAllister, Marvin Edward. *White People Do Not Know How to Behave at Entertainments Designed for Ladies & Gentlemen of Colour*. Chapel Hill: University of North Carolina Press, 2003.

Memoirs of J.H. Payne, the American Roscius: With Criticisms on His Acting. London: John Miller, 1815.

Mencken, H.L. *A Mencken Chrestomathy: His Own Selection of His Choicest Writing*. New York: Vintage, 1982.

———. *Newspaper Days: Mencken's Autobiography: 1899–1906*. Baltimore, MD: Johns Hopkins University Press, 2006.

Merish, Lori. "Melodrama and American Fiction." In *A Companion to American Fiction, 1780–1865*, edited by Shirley Samuels. Malden, MA: Blackwell Publishing, 2004.

Mermaids, Mummies, and Mastodons: The Emergence of the American Museum. Washington, D.C.: American Association of Museums, 1992.

The Mirror of Taste, and Dramatic Censor. Philadelphia, PA: Zantzinger, 1811.

Myers, Robert J., and Joyce Brodowski. "Rewriting the Hallams: Research in 18th Century British and American Theatre." *Theatre Survey* 41, no. 1 (2000): 1–22.

Odell, George C.D. *Annals of the New York Stage*. New York: Columbian University Press, 1927.

Penzel, Frederick. *Theatre Lighting Before Electricity*. Middletown, CT: Wesleyan University Press, 1978.

Planché, James Robinson. *The Recollections and Reflections of J.R. Planché*. London: Tinsley Brothers, 1872.

Power, Tyrone. *Impressions of America: During the Years 1833, 1834, and 1835*. Philadelphia, PA: Carey, Lea & Blanchard, 1836.

Preston, Katherine K. *Opera on the Road: Traveling Opera Troupes in the United States, 1825–60*. Urbana: University of Illinois Press, 1993.

Ranney, H.M. *Account of the Terrific and Fatal Riot at the New-York Astor Place Opera House, On the Night of May 10th, 1849*. New York: H.M. Ranney, 1849.

Ritchey, David. "The Baltimore Fever and the Yellow Fever Epidemic." *Maryland Historical Magazine* 67, no. 3 (Fall 1972): 298-301.

———. *A Guide to the Baltimore Stage in the Eighteenth Century*. Westport, CT: Greenwood Press, 1982.

Roppolo, Joseph P. "Uncle Tom in New Orleans: Three Lost Plays." *New England Quarterly* 27, no. 2 (1954): 213–26.

Sarudy, Barbara Wells. "Genteel and Necessary Amusements: Public Pleasure Gardens in Eighteenth-Century Maryland." *Journal of Garden History* 9, no. 3 (1989): 118–24.

Saxon, Arthur. *Enter Foot and Horse: A History of Hippodrama in England and France*. New Haven, CT: Yale University Press, 1968.

Scharf, John Thomas. *History of Baltimore City and County, from the Earliest Period to the Present Day*. Philadelphia, PA: L.H. Everts, 1881.

Semmes, Raphael. *Baltimore As Seen by Visitors: 1783–1860*. Baltimore: Maryland Historical Society, 1953.

Smith, Gene. *American Gothic*. New York: Simon & Schuster, 1992.

Smith, Ted A. *The New Measures: A Theological History of Democratic Practice*. Cambridge: Cambridge University Press, 2007.

Sollers, John Ford. "The Theatrical Career of John T. Ford." PhD diss., Stanford University, 1962.

Stephen, Lee, and Sidney Lee, eds. *The Dictionary of National Biography*. New York: MacMillan, 1908.

Sutro, Ottilie. "The Wednesday Club: A Brief Sketch from Authentic Sources." *Maryland Historical Magazine* 38, no. 1 (March 1943): 60–68.

Tuckerman, Henry. *The Life of John Pendleton Kennedy*. New York: G.P. Putnum & Sons, 1871.

Tuska, Benjamin. "Know-Nothingism in Baltimore 1854–1860." *Catholic Historical Review* 11, no. 2 (1925): 217–51.

Varle, Charles. *A Complete View of Baltimore*. Baltimore: S. Young, 1833.

Wemyss, Francis Courtney. *Theatrical Biography; or the Life of an Actor and Manager*. Glasgow: R. Griffin, 1848.

———. *Wemyss' Chronology of the American Stage, from 1752–1852*. New York: W.M. Taylor, 1852.

Witham, Barry B., ed. *Theatre in the Colonies and United States*. Vol. 1. *1750–1915*. Cambridge: Cambridge University Press, 1996.

Wood, William Burke. *Personal Recollections of the Stage: Embracing Notices of Actors, Authors, and Auditors, During a Period of Forty Years*. Philadelphia, PA: H.C. Baird, 1855.

Yates, Edmund, ed. *The Life and Correspondence of Charles Mathews, the Elder, Comedian*. London: Routledge, Warne and Routledge, 1860.

NEWSPAPERS

Baltimore and Maryland

Aegis (Bel Air)
Afro-American (Baltimore)
American and Commercial Daily Advertiser (Baltimore)
Baltimore County Union (Towson)
Baltimore Daily Advertiser
Baltimore Daily Commercial
Baltimore Evening Post
Baltimore Evening Sun
Baltimore Sun
Daily Exchange (Baltimore)
Der Deutsche Correspondent (Baltimore)
Maryland Gazette (Annapolis)
Maryland Journal, and the Baltimore Advertiser
National Republican (Washington)
News (Frederick)
Torch Light and Public Advertiser (Hagerstown)

Others

Alexandria Gazette
Chicago Tribune

Commercial Gazette (Cincinnati)
Daily Phoenix (Columbia, SC)
Detroit Free Press
Examiner (London)
Kansas City Times
Los Angeles Times
Morning Post (London)
National Advocate (New York)
National Banner and Nashville Whig
New York Daily Herald
New York Times
Philadelphia Inquirer
Spirit of the Times (New York)
United States Gazette (Philadelphia)
Virginia Argus (Richmond)
World (New York)

INDEX

ABOUT THE AUTHOR

Dr. Charlie Mitchell is an associate professor of theater at the University of Florida, where he teaches history and performance. He is a graduate of Ithaca College, Boston University and the University of Colorado at Boulder. Charlie has worked as an actor and director for a variety of theaters in New York, Chicago, Gainesville and Baltimore, where he was an artistic associate with the award-winning Chesapeake Shakespeare Company. He is the author of *Shakespeare and Public Execution*, the coeditor of *Zora Neale Hurston: Collected Plays* and a contributor and editor of *Theatrical Worlds*, the first open-source introductory theater textbook. He is also the author of several plays, including *The Snow Queen* and *The Report*.